THE STEEP ATLANTICK STREAM

THE STEEP ATLANTICK STREAM

ROBERT HARLING

With drawings by
JOHN WORSLEY

New Introduction by Derek Law

LYONS
PRESS

Essex, Connecticut

An imprint of Globe Pequot, the trade division of
The Rowman & Littlefield Publishing Group, Inc.
4501 Forbes Blvd., Ste. 200
Lanham, MD 20706
www.rowman.com

Distributed by NATIONAL BOOK NETWORK

This edition first published in Great Britain in 2022 by
Seaforth Publishing,
A division of Pen & Sword Books Ltd,
47 Church Street,
Barnsley S70 2AS
www.seaforthpublishing.com

First Lyons Press edition 2023

British Library Cataloguing in Publication Information available

Library of Congress Cataloging-in-Publication Data

Names: Harling, Robert, author. | Worsley, John, illustrator.
Title: The steep Atlantick stream / Robert Harling ; with drawings by John
  Worsley ; new introduction by Derek Law.
Description: First Lyons Press edition. | Essex, Connecticut : Lyons Press, 2023. | "This
  edition first published in Great Britain in 2022 by Seaforth Publishing, A division of
  Pen & Sword Books Ltd, 47 Church Street, Barnsley S70 2AS."— Title page verso. |
  Summary: "First published in 1946, a memoir of the author's experiences during the
  Battle of the Atlantic that offers one of the most original accounts of the war at sea
  in the 'cockleshell corvettes' which faced down the threat of the U-boat menace"—
  Provided by publisher.
Identifiers: LCCN 2023030038 (print) | LCCN 2023030039 (ebook) | ISBN
  9781493076574 (paperback) | ISBN 9781493076581 (epub)
Subjects: LCSH: World War, 1939–1945—Campaigns—Atlantic Ocean. | Harling, Robert.
  | World War, 1939–1945—Personal narratives, British. | World War, 1939–1945—Naval
  operations, British. | Tobias (Corvette) | Great Britain. Royal Naval Volunteer Reserve—
  Biography.
Classification: LCC D771 .H337 2023 (print) | LCC D771 (ebook) | DDC
  940.54/5941092—dc23/eng/20230627
LC record available at https://lccn.loc.gov/2023030038
LC ebook record available at https://lccn.loc.gov/2023030039

Contents

The Star that bids the Shepherd fold,
Now the top of Heav'n doth hold,
And the gilded Car of Day,
His glowing Axle doth allay
In the steep Atlantick stream,
And the slope Sun his upward beam
Shoots against the dusky Pole,
Pacing toward the other gole
Of his Chamber in the East.

COMUS: *A Masque*
John Milton

New Introduction

By Derek Law

M ost naval autobiographical works published during the Second World War or at war's end are tales of derring-do, of fighting off U-boat attacks on convoys, of famous raids and battles, of bravery against all the odds. They were often written by professional Royal Navy officers. But there is also a small handful of hidden and neglected gems written by RNVR officers and volunteers who led full professional lives before and after the war and who describe the novelty of their wartime naval experiences and life – a life full of boredom and fatigue, of fear and fun with rare spells of action. Ludovic Kennedy's *Sub-Lieutenant* describes such a life in Home Fleet destroyers; Peter Scott's *The Eye of the Wind* is mainly about his service in Coastal Forces; Godfrey Winn's account of his experiences on Arctic convoys and Nicholas Monsarrat's wartime works about his service in corvettes, frigates and destroyers all capture that sense of months of boredom and routine punctuated by moments of extreme terror.

To complete the small list of books which capture perfectly the spirit of the time one should certainly add the best but probably the least known of these gems, Robert Harling's work *The Steep Atlantick Stream* now back in print for the first time in fifty years.

Harling was a polymath. An influential typographer with a hugely successful professional career, he was a prolific author throughout his life as well as having an astonishingly varied and successful wartime career. On his death in 2008 he was described in a *Times* obituary as 'the most innovative and distinguished typographer of the last century'. He was born in 1910 and grew up with a love of art and architecture and even published two books on these themes before the war. By 1939 he had established a growing reputation as an expert on typography and it was in that year that he first met Ian Fleming, who was to become a lifelong friend. Fleming had admired his work as editor of the journal *Typography* and commissioned Harling to redesign the Admiralty's weekly intelligence report. It would then be almost two years before they met again.

Harling was a keen amateur sailor who quickly volunteered for the Royal Navy, where he very soon found himself at Dunkirk in charge of a whaler. This prompted him to write the much acclaimed semi-autobiographical book *Amateur Sailor*, published in 1944 under the pseudonym of Nicholas Drew. It was praised by the Poet Laureate John Masefield as the best eyewitness account of Dunkirk ever written.

After Dunkirk and now a Sub-Lieutenant, Harling next found himself serving on a corvette on convoy duty in the North Atlantic. Then following a meeting with Ian Fleming in London in 1941 he was recruited to work in the Inter-Service Topographical Department (ISTD), where his role was the analysis of aerial photographs of enemy held territory. The following year Fleming set up 30 AU (30 Assault Unit) a secret marine commando unit which was very much his private army and tasked with operating on and ahead of the front line to recover enemy code-books, security documents and wireless equipment. He recruited Harling as one of his team charged with playing the key role of the link between 30 AU, where the marines knew him as Fleming's 'head boy', and the Naval Intelligence Division led by Fleming himself. At that time the journalist Sefton Delmer and another friend of Fleming described Harling as 'a young man with the laughing, big-eared, long-nosed face of a medieval court jester and the shrewd appraising eyes of a physician'. Harling and Fleming were to remain close friends throughout their lives and he even had his name used in Fleming's novel *Thunderball* as Nassau Commissioner of Police Harling and also in the *The Spy who Loved Me* as a typesetter. Indeed Harling's last published work only appeared in 2015 and is a personal and frank biography and memoir of Ian Fleming. Harling's war continued its remarkable trajectory, working with 30 AU in France including a memorable meeting with General George Patton, followed by a dramatic dash across Germany to Magdeburg to round up German scientists. He then ended his war with a visit to Norway to help disarm German naval forces.

The Steep Atlantick Stream – the title coming from a quotation by John Milton – is a perfect example of his fluid, well-paced and engaging writing style. It is again a semi-autobiographical work which describes his experiences first in the London Blitz, then travelling by troopship to New York, then standing by a corvette being built in Canada, of learning the skills of his new role as First Lieutenant and building relationships with his captain, his fellow officers and crew. It then describes their individual and collective experience as they range the Atlantic from Nova Scotia to the Clyde and from Iceland to Freetown. There are descriptions of convoy battles where his ship is sometimes at the centre and sometimes at the edge of the action, but above all it focuses on the personal experiences of the randomly thrown together group who inhabit the wardroom and the men who live and work below deck. It tells of the dominance of Atlantic weather, of visits to new and exotic ports, of time spent on shore leave in Iceland and at sea with a friend on an East Coast MTB flotilla, of the forming of a close working relationship with his captain, of wardroom parties and of weeks spent at sea.

He is able to stand back and use his broad and lucid vocabulary and sensitive and witty style to describe the challenges faced by new young officers learning new skills whether technical or personal, realising that the lives of the crew might depend on their competence. He captures the spirit of the mixed group of new and seasoned ABs and Petty Officers drawn from different classes and regional backgrounds and how they learn to work together. Although there are descriptions of many naval actions these events are almost peripheral to the core of the book which captures the role of individuals in creating a community which will endure the tests of life at sea with dogged determination. Harling writes with a well-paced and engaging style which captures the conversation and dialogue of the time with a vivid and realistic style. Some of the language of those days, whether describing interactions with the local population in Freetown or relations between men and women is very much of its time, but in a sense this shows him catching the cultural climate of the 1940s – very different from the cultural climate of today – but undeniably vibrant and closely observed.

Harling swiftly adjusted to civilian life and re-established himself in a whole range of activities. He remained a prolific author, writing half a dozen well-received novels in the 1950s and 1960s, many based in Fleet Street, and non-fiction works about the artist and typeface designer Eric Gill and the artist and engraver Tirzah Ravilious. He was soon based in Fleet Street himself and from 1957 he worked in journalism with an astonishing 36-year tenure between 1957 and 1993 editing *House & Garden*, but also working at different times in senior roles on *The Sunday Times*, where he was architectural correspondent as well as a typographical consultant designer.

The Steep Atlantick Stream has one other remarkable component. Each chapter heading has a small drawing with a relevant naval theme drawn by the official war artist John

Worsley, a pre-war commercial artist who had joined the Royal Navy in 1939 and spent three years serving on convoy escorts in the Atlantic. His pictures of life on board ship were soon acquired by the War Artists Advisory Committee (WAAC), and he was made an official war artist. In 1943, he was captured in the Mediterranean and spent the rest of the war in a naval prison camp, Marlag 'O' near Bremen in Germany. Worsley continued to record the war while in captivity using artistic supplies from the Red Cross. Worsley and Harling then briefly worked together after the war ended.

This is a classic, absorbing and realistic work which more than almost any other Second World War naval memoir leaves the reader with an unforgettable impression of what the war at sea was really like for those who served in the small ships, almost continually facing the enemy, rather than serving their time in fleet anchorages awaiting action.

Derek Law

Chapter 1
Word of *Tobias*

Two years ago, during a time of leave in London, I went to watch the Sadlers Wells Ballet at the New Theatre, and heard Mr Robert Helpmann declaim a passage from *Comus*, in the ballet designed for that masque. Four of the words from that declamation were held in my mind, and have been much with me since. The words, *the steep Atlantick stream,* seemed to me beautiful and more, for they seemed also to contain a picture more clear and sharp than many words could make, of that ocean which I came to know so well; and I remember that I returned to my home and to my bookshelves and took out a forgotten Milton and turned to the lines, reading them with pleasure; gaining pleasure, too, in the retention of the final 'k' as in an Elizabethan chart. Thus I have kept the words against this time when I might begin once more to write a book, hearing in my mind the sonorous words, and seeing *Atlantick* always with this typographical affectation. Perhaps

1

I have too great presumption borrowing these words, but it is certain that none of my own could make a title as pleasing to my ears and eyes, and so, an hour ago, I wrote the words at the head of this page.

Yet starting this project, I am gloomy indeed, for here, in Alexandria, the evening is lustrous, and there would be more pleasure going out to Ramleh to dine with friends, or to go later to watch the cabaret at the Carlton, or even to walk along the Corniche, than set to writing, despite a resolution I made this morning that I should fill this page of His Majesty's foolscap before I slept tonight. The four words are insistent; they intrude, even here, into this world of colour and sun. If I should leave this rickety table and cross to the balcony which overlooks the vast deserted eastern harbour, I should see the memorable blues of the Mediterranean, yet I remain instead with these four words which have become a theme for so many of my thoughts and now this book. Even in writing them the grey clouds of the Western Ocean seem at once more real than the corner of blue sky I see from this chair; reading them I recall more easily the grimed wharves of Halifax than spacious quays I trod last week in Haifa; and lava slopes in Iceland are more vividly remembered than the hills of Lebanon. I often wonder why those harsh seas should claim memory so abidingly, but this is a query that has pestered many mariners and will perhaps persist through life and maybe has no answer.

Now I have filled my foolscap; I have made my preface or perhaps my apologia and I can defer until tomorrow, next week, next month or even next year, the beginning of my book.

꧁

I remember that I left the Captain and the First Lieutenant of *Solander,* my first ship in this war, standing upon a Belfast quay. They turned away, undoubtedly to return to the pleasantries of the Grand Central Hotel, as I climbed on board the Irish cross-channel steamer and went below, to my bunk. I was sad, and sadness remained with me throughout the passage to the Clyde. I had enjoyed life in *Solander,* and the prospect of change was unwelcome to me, as to most Englishmen; I had no desire to join a new ship, and could have wished that Their Lordships might have partnered me in this desire. My sombre mood had, too, another more commonplace reason, for, after the buffeting corvette, my berth in the soberly-throbbing steamer was no sedative, but kept me wakeful, prompting many ponderings.

Those doubts which had dominated my earlier journey to that East Riding port to join *Solander* were again insistent. It was true that I could now claim practical experience as a professional mariner, and, I glibly told myself, as 'a junior executive officer', but I doubted whether six months of winter warfare had given me sufficient experience to take as First Lieutenant to a new corvette. I might (and did) gaze for strength and comfort to the two bright, gold, wavy bands of braid around the sleeve of my reefer, draped upon a chair, but the braid held no answers to the questions I now posed so glumly to myself. Once more I was subdued by self-doubts, although I smiled, perhaps somewhat smugly, to note the technical background which now shadowed the questions. Six months before, I had doubted whether I could take a ship into a darkened roadstead to gain a signalled berth. I believed that now I might accomplish this task, but asked again whether I should have enough of what Their Lordships so icily termed 'officer-like qualities' to control the working lives of a crew of sixty men. Before, I had been sceptical of the results of my academic navigation in a dull day in mid-Atlantic. Now I was dubiously confident that my dead reckoning would get a ship through, but tempered that confidence with a recital of the new tasks for which I should soon be responsible; for ammunition totals, pay records and allotments, signals, the confidence and confidences of a crew, depth charge records, initial stores and replacements of stores, a library of 'Confidential', 'Secret', and 'Most Secret' documents and code books, and for the thousand-and-one other items which would help to make and keep the ship 'in all respects ready for war'. Nominally these were the Captain's responsibilities, but in practice they are apt to become the First Lieutenant's own, and I shivered, turning again in my too-comfortable bunk. Sleepless, I rose early to dress and shave; and climbed on deck to evade the devil in my mind.

The passage through the Clyde, from Gourock up to Glasgow, was heartening; this was the first time I had made the passage beyond Greenock and the sight of the vast forces being assembled in that long shipbuilding corridor was impressive enough to make a sailor wish to cheer. Two officers of the Polish Army were obviously discussing this embryonic power. One was short, middle-aged, voluble and as teutonic in appearance as many other Polish officers I had seen. The other was young and handsome, and attentive to the views of his senior. The older man suddenly turned towards me, to invoke my aid as commentator in this journey between the slipways of the Clyde. I remembered a friend who had once labelled a phrase-proud BBC star as 'that detestable describer', and steeled myself for an equally thankless role.

'That,' I said, as he pointed to a hull braced between skeletal stocks, 'is a merchantman. About five thousand tons.'

The word 'merchantman' was puzzling to the younger Pole, and I corrected my description to 'merchant ship'.

'What is it that she carries?' he asked.

'General cargo,' I explained, but realised quickly that this phrase, too, was weak, puzzling to them both, for their brows contracted in an effort to place the Spanish-sounding hero I had named. I tried again. This was going to be tricky, I thought.

'Anything: motors, tanks, food, aeroplanes on deck if she has space.'

They nodded, but the next inquiry was as difficult; we were passing a destroyer lying in the stream; a great gap yawned in her bows, and the older man said, 'What is that?'

I said 'that' was a destroyer, but was questioned more precisely. What had happened to her? Had she been in battle? or a collision? or mined? It was difficult to say, I weakly replied: perhaps she had been mined, possibly torpedoed; one could not say with certainty. They agreed. The fact that the ship was still afloat impressed them. I was also impressed, for the fo'c'sle head supported itself for a length of forty feet above the void where bow waves had once chopped against steel plates. The plates which remained were twisted and mis-shapen as if some giant hand had gripped them in frenzy. My companions were silent for a while, meditating perhaps upon the damaged ship and the fate of her crew. Then they were quickened into curiosity concerning a small gunboat or destroyer lying alongside one of the quays and flying the Netherlands flag and the White Ensign. She was a beautiful craft, and I wished momentarily that corvettes could be built with such swift steel lines. I had a vague memory of having seen a photograph in *Jane's Fighting Ships* of a similar ship of the *torpedobooten* class. She was perhaps about the same gross tonnage as *Solander*, but against the corvette's beamy whaling lines she would have looked a lean and lovely but fragile craft, and I could easily imagine the very small change she would have got from Lieutenant-Commander Jack Dickens, RNR, had we been deputed to work with her as sister ship in convoy escort work, and how, on the bridge, we should have been moved to disparaging comment upon her prospects in a mid-Atlantic cyclone. Yet she was an impressive craft, and my eyes followed round as we left her astern.

The rest of the journey was a pitiless cross-examination of my seafaring ignorance. I comforted myself with the hope that my companions knew less than myself, and with the reflection that if, by chance, I was engaging in careless talk, my hazy information was scarcely likely to prove of use to any enemy agent; rather the reverse, in fact. As we docked and I moved to go below to get my gear I received two clipped, impeccable salutes. These I returned in a manner worthy, I hoped, of His Majesty the King, the Royal Navy, and the rasp-voiced Chief Petty Officer, who had, so many months before, explained the niceties of the naval salute to thirty sub-lieutenants on the lawn alongside the training 'ship' *King Alfred:* 'Palm straight! *And* flat! *And* at an angle of forty-five degrees to the 'orizontal deck! *And* none of your cack-'anded, flat-'anded, yessir, three-bags-full-sir, army-style jokes! Now, imagine I'm Admiral of the Fleet Sir Dudley Pound 'isself just coming aboard ... CLASS! SALUTE!'

~&

Sunday Glasgow was a fitting background to my mood. We disembarked on a deserted quay in an outlandish part of the city. Few taximen ventured near the wharves and warehouses, and when a solitary driver cruised along he was surrounded by a crowd of his countrymen, and in such a foray I knew that Sassenachs stood no chance. After ten minutes two other taxis came to explore the quay-side street, and in company with the two Polish officers I seized upon one of these and thus made my way into Glasgow, to St Enoch's Station.

(Surely, amongst the major and discordant memories of any traveller to or from the wars must be recollections of baggage. It is certain that no peacetime luggage was so cumbersome, possessed of such deadweight or was packed into such awkward shapes. I travel more lightly than most sailors, yet my suitcase and seabag were heavy, unmanageable, maddening. I lugged them from the taxi to the baggage office. The seabag knocked against my ankles, the suitcase against my shins, my bridge coat twisted around my knees, my respirator swung against my haunches. I was dispirited and unreasonable, and deposited my bags into the care of the London, Midland and Scottish Railway with venomous relief.)

From the baggage office I went swiftly to the office for sleeper reservations, counted myself amongst the world's favoured mortals to gain a third-class sleeper at such short notice, and then went for an early lunch to one of the few Glaswegian restaurants which, by merely remaining open, defied the bleak conventions of the northern sabbath.

⤙❧

Twenty-four hours later I made my first official visit to the Admiralty. As an amateur in architecture I had often, in more peaceful days, noted with approval that eighteenth-century facade which the brothers Adam had designed for the delight of London perambulators and Their Lords Commissioners. Now I passed beyond that gallery and screen, with its exuberantly sculptured seahorses, into the cobbled quadrangle which fronts the main, earlier building. A four-ring captain, RN, preceded me; he had descended from a taxi and walked past the sentries, displaying with a casual gesture what I imagined to be an Admiralty pass. I coveted the casual touch, for I could merely display the rather limp and dirty copy of the signal I had been given in Northern Ireland, but the Royal Marine policeman was friendly and pointed to the swing doors which lead to the Holy Place. The captain, again waving his pass, was crossing the blackand-white chequered tile floor (ought one to write 'deck'? I think I shall never discard this landlubber's usage for that of the professional seaman). Two other officers were standing before a high desk. Behind the desk were two commissionaires, apparently seated on Dickensian high stools. One of the officers, a lieutenant-commander, RN, could not recall the correct title of the department or division he wished to visit. The other, a commander, also RN, was behaving in a genially fussy manner, obviously pleased with himself, the world, the purpose and prospects of his visit. I stood by the open fire opposite the desk. Three messenger girls, dressed in dark blue aprons, were also warming themselves, chattering in what they probably considered to be offstage whispers.

The focal point of the hall of the Admiralty is a statue of Nelson placed in a niche facing the double swing doors and the Whitehall courtyard. I examined the statue: a legend on the plinth records that the statue is a copy of Bailey's original model on the column in Trafalgar Square. The hall has an air of remoteness from the twentieth century and inevitably thoughts move in evocation of the many famous and unknown seamen, from Nelson to Captain Scott, from Beatty to oneself, who have waited in this hall, fretting to be called to senior officers, to hear of new appointments; and then, my thoughts drifting scandalously, I could not escape from the impression that I had been translated through the years, back to my early youth, and that these were the boldly-patterned black-and-white tiles which had embellished my Uncle Taff's South Coast dairy. In such untrammelled ways does an undisciplined mind career, even in the most augustan surroundings. Indeed, my mind was engaged by these memories when one of the messengers was called upon to escort the commander upon his errand, and I stepped forward to show my signal to one of the commissionaires. He had one arm and a white, pointed beard in the manner of Field-Marshal Smuts. He was, I imagined, the famous Mr Jewell whose portrait I had seen reproduced in a *Picture Post* feature article dealing with life in the Admiralty. After scanning the message he directed me to another Admiralty establishment, 'five minutes away, just up Regent Street'.

Thus brief was my first visit to the Admiralty! I went out into Whitehall and walked towards Piccadilly. The spring morning was cold and sharp, a morning when Portland stone and blue skies are the most apposite urban companions in the world, when London is almost beautiful. I wondered whether *Solander*, with her new junior officer, would be at sea yet, but put such thoughts aside as irrelevant to this moment of freedom and walked up Haymarket as zestfully as a Regency buck.

❧

An interview with the lieutenant-commander, RNVR, in charge of Appointments, Reserve Officers, was also brief. I was to go to a new corvette, building in Canada. I would go in a fast convoy to New York, thence to Halifax; or to Halifax direct and report to the naval base. There I should be told the location of the yard in which the ship was building and receive further travelling orders if necessary. He was sorry he could not be more precise in direction; corvettes were being built throughout Canada. I would get sailing orders and details concerning port of embarkation and times of departure in about ten days from the Ministry of War Transport. Meanwhile I had seven days' leave, but they could probably be lengthened to eight or nine if all my gear could be packed and ready. From now on I was out of his hands; all future inquiries should be made to the Ministry of War Transport.

'The name of my ship?' I queried.

'It's here, I think. Yes, *Tobias,* corvette. She ought to be quite a good berth. I suppose you're fairly well acquainted with their parlour tricks by now.'

I agreed. There were other questions, mainly about gear for Canada, and whether he thought I would be returning for Atlantic duties, Far East or Mediterranean work.

'There's nothing here about tropical kit. There usually is if anybody's going East. You can take it that she'll probably come back here. Probably be the same run you've been doing.'

In some ways that was relief. Transitions have always been suspect to my mind. Even the North Atlantic could become a habit to be preferred to the unknown qualities of the Pacific or Mediterranean, although once or twice I had thought that I should like to see something of the North African war.

There was relief, too, in the thought of continuing service in corvettes. They had been designed in a hurry, I often thought, clutching at the handrail on the bridge in times of unseasonable weather. They were ugly, uncomfortable, confined; condemned always to routine duties as 'wet nurses to old merchantmen', as my Captain had once said. In their squat, lumbering way they did their dual duty as convoy protectors and U-boat chasers. With their modest armament they tried fiercely to threaten venturesome enemy planes. At inadequate speeds they pursued, often relentlessly, sometimes successfully, the most efficient U-boats the Germans could send into our sea lanes. They were improvised craft, amateurish in appearance, and often amateur in conduct. Those who served in them could never look upon them with undue approval or excitement, could never seize the arms of land-loving friends, impelled to say, 'Look, there is my ship. Is she not a beauty?' Instead, we gazed upon our craft silently, perhaps with affection, certainly in deprecation, as if regarding some venerable mastiff grown solid and slow in long and faithful service.

From such a ship I had come: to such a ship I was now directed. Yet secretly, I was relieved. The glamorous ships of the Royal Navy also had their drawbacks, I had heard and, like most mortals, I preferred demerits of the thousand-tonner I knew to those of unknown County Class cruisers or battlewagons.

I placed my new orders (contained upon one half-sheet of flimsy paper) importantly in my notecase. The most urgent matter was to get to North Wales as quickly as possible. I was wishful for green hills after months of the green Atlantic. I would stay in London on Saturday and Sunday, I decided, and journey to Wales over Sunday night, for he is an unwise traveller who arrives at the edge of Snowdonia on Sunday. No buses or cars travel in those devout or perhaps lazy communities on that day of rest; the seclusion of the mountain villages is complete. So I stayed in Fleet Street, my obliging tenant Stephen returning once more, upon my sudden request, to his mother's house in Surrey.

∿

I have been told often, since that evening, that I should insider myself lucky to have experienced the greatest of the many air raids made upon London by the Luftwaffe, 'especially,' my congratulators affirm, 'in Fleet Street, of all places!', but I have long considered that experience of ferocity and fury is usually of dubious value. Certainly one learns to grip and subdue certain primeval reactions to fear; but if this growth in knowledge for two million people is deemed worth the killing and maiming of a score, my values are questionable and heretical. I some times tire to hear the shibboleths of the 'purification through suffering' school of thought. We never saw signs of spiritual grandeur upon the brows of broken seamen we helped from petrol-blazing seas. Most people –

civilians or warriors – suffer pain and sorrow stoically; few crack and few emerge from suffering as more saintly creatures, purified by pain. German citizens suffered bombings as firmly as the British; presumably they, too, by these same tokens, gained in spiritual grandeur, but I never heard this theory given credence. These, however, are controversial subjects and perhaps have no place in the records of an amateur sailor. I will have done and return to my tale ...

I was reading when the alert wailed into the quietened week-end world of Fleet Street. I had heard the alert fewer times than the average Londoner and its direful summons still held novelty. I read for some time but becoming oppressed by the confines of my room, the noise of bombs and the barrage, I went out. The caretaker, old and gentle, was climbing and puffing his way to the roof. He said: 'I think this is going to be a real one, sir. You'll be wishing you was back at sea!'

That was already my wish. To be bombed at sea seems always safer than to be amongst bricks and mortar, slabs of concrete, lengths of girder. Such architectural oddments are so solid, seem likely to fall with such finality, throwing death and dismemberment about with casual confusion and profusion. It is certain that most sailors would agree with this view. I walked out of the courtway into Fetter Lane. A great hose was being unwound from a Fleet Street hydrant, coiling slowly and cumbrously like a great distended boa. Long-fingered fires already reached from burning buildings to grip office blocks, sought tentative holds, tightened and then gripped. Firemen worked like maniacal saviours. I joined a local firefighting unit which was tackling a blaze on the top floor of an office building in Fetter Lane. The work was exciting, but the unrelenting one-sidedness of the attack made any Atlantic U-boat battle an affair of sporting exchanges between well-matched opponents.

We worked through the long night, trying to fight against fires and bombs with sand and inadequate water supplies. In the early morning, water was exhausted. Then we watched from a rooftop. Flames caught and fired building after building until the whole city seemed ablaze. The spectacle was unreal. One could not comprehend that the firing of a great capital was actually happening before one's eyes. I remember this sensation of unreality as a dominant impression of the night. Fear came only when we stopped working, when an adjacent roof fell in, or when the long chain of firefighters, bucket-fillers and bucket-passers paused owing to a breakdown in the water system. Then the screaming crescendo of bombs made us cower, become shrinking creatures, aware of death or, far worse, dreadful injury. We crouched as the crashes came. Often they were near and the building rocked. At such times death seemed unlikely to miss oneself, and I wished again, intensely, that I was back at sea.

Afterwards, recalling these sensations, I tried to examine this wish. At sea, in moments of tension, a common purpose grips and strengthens a crew. Their ship, their little world, is a tangible reality, having unity. Against that world fear may impinge, but the impact is dulled; the unity is too strong to buckle. Leadership still further strengthens this unity; also the fact that each man must work. In city streets, however, the world is spread around: vast, diffused, unmanageable. People are separate, remote from each other, and, therefore, weaker. An air raid shelter does not move, fight, live like a ship. It is static and must wait, and waiting weakens the will. After reasoning along these lines I am more than ever convinced of an essential sanity at that time in wishing to be back at sea.

The 'all-clear' shrilled just before six o'clock in the morning. There was little more that we could do as firefighters. Even the real firemen were defeated by lack of water. The eastern side of Fetter Lane was almost wholly afire. A northern wind carried flames across the narrow streets, catching and gripping upper storeys as if swung upon fiendish trapezes. Shoe Lane was also aflame. Inevitably our small block of flats would be caught in this converging inferno, but resentment against the Luftwaffe seemed crushed in weariness. I was glad to be a temporary London flat-dweller, and not a London fireman, and, with this thought, climbed to my home, and fell upon my bed, intending to sleep until told to go.

The caretaker rang at eight o'clock to say that we had been given ten minutes to get our stuff into the courtyard, for the building was doomed. There was still no water, and the wind had carried the fire to an office building at the end of the cul-de-sac. I moved gloomily about my room, taking half-a-dozen books and my blankets; that was all.

I read some months later an account from Berne which purported to give an eye-witness record of Berliners who had no seeming wish to try to gain any possessions from the debris of their homes. I now understand the apathy of those creatures bombed into insensibility by incessant RAF raids. I think, too, that the truth of this statement could be verified by those who were in Plymouth or Coventry when those cities were heavily bombed. One is alive; one wishes only for sleep and food. These are the elemental things. A piece of Staffordshire china, a rug, a painting, an armchair endeared by the years, seem insubstantial things. Perhaps this is a universal reaction, for other residents appeared with almost oriental assortments of dresses and suits yet made no effort to drag furniture into the courtyard. Among my six books, I noticed Lewis Mumford's *The Culture of Cities*, but I cannot think this was seized upon as a textbook for a future metropolitan world.

We laughed and chatted, for there is invariably a sardonic member of any impromptu group. One said he had never been able to get his own fire going so quickly or so early on a Sunday morning; another that we should pass a vote of thanks to the caretaker, the only one amongst us who had not retired to sleep at six o'clock, or else we might have slept and become cinders, but the caretaker did not smile and shook his head sadly and shuffled once more to the doorway to help a tenant, a woman journalist, with her portable typewriter.

Then, suddenly, the wind swung round, almost through 180 degrees. I had been susceptible to the movement of the breeze through the courtyard, watching its control of the smoke. An eddy, I thought, caught by the structure of the courtyard. A fireman had also noted the change (momentarily later than a sailor, I preened myself) and called from the rooftop that there might yet be a chance, and water came once more from the hydrants, and our homes were saved.

Such a conclusion may seem novelettish, but it was the sober climax or anti-climax to our night. Perhaps some of us felt guilty to return to our rooms when so many buildings were enflamed. I cannot tell; I wished only for sleep, and thought that if this had been a miracle it was a pleasant intervention of divinity, but then again, in scepticism, wondered why the miracle had not come five minutes before and saved the buildings of the more valuable printshop and the printing-ink manufacturer upon the corners of the adjacent alley, but some are never satisfied. That I learned long ago, and, for minds too curious, and for those without faith, I have been told, there is no true understanding in this world.

~&~

During Sunday afternoon I walked up Fetter Lane towards Euston Station to get a ticket for the overnight train. The roped-off streets were desolate in a manner too well remembered by many millions of Londoners to need words in these pages. Broken glass lay thickly upon the road. Gaunt and grimy firemen jerked hose pipes into order; others still worked upon smouldering buildings. Only a few sightseers came to this backwater and a police sergeant let me through. I said, obviously enough, that it had been a bad night.

'Think we can write most of Fetter Lane off,' he said, 'and further east they've had it worse. Still, they'll get it back with interest one of these days!'

I picked my way through glass and rubble. The loathsome smell of burning could not be evaded. Smoke drifted into the eyes. The city seemed parched and dying, tired beyond endurance or even the desire to endure, yet the few Londoners I saw, although tired, seemed resilient within their own strange cheerfulness. This resistance, I thought, walking towards King's Cross, was not something articulate, taught upon the playing-fields or within the form-rooms of upstage schools. These people could never see this high quality in themselves and when told of their courage by admiring New York journalists, they regarded their informants wryly, not understanding. I persuaded myself that an admixture of Welsh and Irish bloods enabled me to remain impersonal in these high-flown thoughts upon the English: it was at least one way of making bearable the walk along the sordid stretch of Gray's Inn Road.

❦

I spent my days in Wales. The transition from the Atlantic to London, thence to the quiet hills seemed as swift as the changes of backcloth in a melodrama. I could liken Hebog, Yr Aran or Snowdon itself to a peaceful 'curtain', but I knew well that these hills and valleys, mountain tracks and pools could be likened more truthfully to a set of beguiling lantern slides, suitable perhaps to an interval, but certainly no more than that.

❦

Instructions for my journey followed me to Wales. I came down to breakfast on my second morning in the mountainside hotel to find a bulky packet of official forms, details, warnings and baggage labels. I noted the code characters of my convoy and, most important of all, that I still had a week's grace.

'I have to acquaint you,' announced the letter, stamped redly and hugely SECRET, 'that first-class passage to enable you to take up your appointment has been arranged. No steamer ticket is required before embarkation in this country, but this communication should be produced if necessary to the Divisional Sea Transport Officer.' I was also informed, with that actuarial touch inseparable from British official communication, that I was entitled to convey 'free of charge, 6 cwt or 30 cubic feet, at 5 cubic feet to the cwt, of baggage'.

I was also informed:

... that American Head Tax would not be payable (and wondered what American Head Tax might possibly be);

... that I must surrender my camera 'at the time of embarkation to the master of the ship who will retain it in his possession throughout the voyage';

... that 'no mention whatsoever should be made concerning the composition of any convoy or the routeing or destination of any convoy or ship';

... that I should have to get permission through my bankers 'to take any of the following out of the country: gold, securities or policies';

... a score of other details concerning customs, finance, firearms, security, censorship, exit permits, sleepers and so on and so on.

My breakfast was a pleasurable meal; on every page of the closely-typed sheets were many smiles. The copious instructions had been prepared, it seemed, as an admonition to cunning magnates with vast securities in this country, desperate to slip to the United States with wealth and cameras secreted about their persons, and voluble with indiscretions concerning their errand. I would look carefully at fellow passengers and help the Minister of War Transport in his onerous task, I decided, and indulging what my Uncle Taff had always called a 'cheap sense of humour', I buttered my toast, buoyant at the prospect of enlivening dull days as a passenger in one of those convoys I had so often watched from *Solander*'s bridge.

❧

The last two days of my leave passed in a fashion now become familiar as a routine for latter days of leave: I made farewells of friends, saw two plays, packed and repacked my bags (computing them at not more than a total of five cubic feet) and waited, growing restless and nervous as the day of my departure neared. Always I wish to go away, and always as the day approaches, wish to stay, love of habit and foreboding placed in uneasy balance. Once more I gave the flat back to the keeping of my obliging tenant, and once more went, his wish that I might find the Atlantic extremely dry a typical farewell.

I was to leave London by the overnight train. I had been promised a sleeper by an optimistic railway clerk and reached Euston early in an attempt to confirm his optimism and viewed approvingly my name upon that list of fortunates pasted upon the coach door. The name was ticked by the steward. I deposited my bags and wandered off to have a cup of sandy coffee.

Euston, under its dreary yellow lights, was milling with that medley of humanity which seems reserved for the circus, the racecourse and railway station. Here the medley was mainly martial. Sailors moved along the platform, the arms of some locked around the waists of godspeeding wives and sweethearts, the arms of others locked less lovingly around gigantic seabags. Soldiers swigged their final cups of tea outside the buffet. Brass-hats sauntered, remote and glassy-eyed, towards the sleepers. (At least, remoteness seemed to cling to them until the moment they espied a porter; then, on the instant, they were as fussy as old maids in a Cheltenham crescent. Why, I wondered, are so many of these creatures who command our destinies upon a battlefield or battleship with the equanimity of Wellington or Beatty, so frequently helpless when placed in charge exclusively of themselves in pursuit of a first-class sleeper?)

Wartime partings crowded the platform. I was glad to have no part to play in a similar pair or group, for stations have always seemed to me unsuitable backgrounds for serious partings or even lighter farewells. I have rarely seen signs of enjoyment upon the faces of honeymoon couples despatched publicly and vociferously upon their fond adventures. Perhaps they are appropriate places for the farewells of tycoons who must continue to give instructions to respectful minions until the moment that the train moves from the station, but it is certain they are not places for the partings of sad lovers and unhappy warriors. The fascination of these farewells eludes me, and I cannot think that many men enjoy them. Perhaps they appeal to some universal and masochistic streak in women. I have seen women throw themselves in frenzy upon the platform at Scutari, bidding farewells to husbands and sons off on three-day marketing trips to Ankara, and I have seen a Brooklyn blonde most tearful in Grand Central Station, but I have rarely seen their menfolk enjoying the experience. Perhaps, on the other hand, I lack the tender touch.

I went back to my sleeper, got out my sleeping kit and then opened the first volume of the Everyman edition of *War and Peace*. I had once essayed this mighty task during a climbing holiday, but had then decided that it required an occasion in time and space when one might be pinioned, powerless to escape into the attractions of the outer world. Now such an occasion was at hand, but the moment of beginning I again put off. I took up the *Evening Standard* instead and read a paragraph from the *Londoner's Diary,* but the impressions of the station and the life of London were too close about me, and, restless, I moved once more to the window to look upon the gloomy attractions of a great London station, and there remained until whistles shrilled along the platform and the train stirred heavily into movement.

❧

My journey to the North was complicated only by baggage. The following morning I reported to the appropriate authorities and was directed to a tender lying alongside the quay. Other sailors and many army and RAF officers also climbed on board. We stood about, aimless and curious, looking out on the grey life of the Clyde. We were not to sail in convoy but in a 'Monster', independently.

Chapter 2

Towards *Tobias*

The Great Liner lay out in the stream. That three-funnelled silhouette which, if sighted in the Atlantic, would have brought the blood pumping to the temples of any U-boat commander was an arrogant cynosure for all watchers from the banks of the Clyde. I wondered why the enemy did not send a hundred planes to try to stay the legendary journeys of this great ship about the world. It was certain that German Intelligence would know by some means that once more the *Queen Mary* (or the *QM* as she was invariably known in her martial career) was in the Clyde, and now awaiting once again its usual westward cargo of brass-hats and lesser officers, RAF and Fleet Air Arm trainees; commercial magnates, economic experts, politicians, mail and exports too rare to be entrusted to the slower ways of convoy. Air reconnaissance would have provided details. In the tender we pondered this query. Why

had Hitler never sent a fleet of torpedo-bombers against the
QM or the *QE?* asked an airman.

'Probably because he's a landsman, and doesn't realise
that we can shift a whole division across the Atlantic or from
here to the Indian Ocean in one of 'em,' said a lieutenant-
commander, RN, and there seemed truth and more than
mere opinion in his theory.

'I doubt whether we'd allow the old Hun to go on using
such damned great troop carriers if he had 'em,' said another.
'We'd at least have a crack at settling them.'

'Can't think why he's left 'em alone,' mused a Royal Marine
colonel. 'Surely his Intelligence people tip him the wink.'

'I suppose several U-boat commanders have spotted 'em
at one time or another,' said another, 'but I imagine it's not
much good unless you're dead in the path of a ship as fast as
a Monster.'

'They do say the old *QM's* had a tin-fish under her tail,'
said another.

'They always do say,' said the colonel succinctly and
gossip died.

We looked towards the ship which seemed to lie athwart
the stream, dwarfing all other craft, even tonnage of most
impressive proportions.

'She's not as beautiful as the *Rex* or the *Bremen* but I'd
rather be in her for this trip than either of 'em,' said the
lieutenant-commander. The others began to compare her
with other liners they had known.

I sensed that we all agreed and not only for patriotic
reasons, for she looked an imposing, self-assured giant. Her
record, too, was certainly more reassuring than all the words
that marine architects or engineers might proffer concerning
speed and performance. In a terrible war she had crossed and
recrossed the seas of the world, bringing relief at desperate
moments to struggling armies. She had proved herself a

fortunate warrior, and sailors, amateur and professional, have a disposition to link their own fortunes with those of fortunate ships.

Cruisers, destroyers and an aircraft carrier lay also in the stream, but we knew that none of these men-o'-war would attend us in our passage. The Monster would sail independently, that assignment desired by every skipper. Peremptory orders and a sudden hobnailed clatter on the quayside broke our speculations. Then silence. We moved to the rail to inquire. A file of German prisoners was coming aboard under the brooding gaze of a self-conscious corporal. He stood guard at the gangway, a tommy-gun at the ready.

'German merchant seamen. A raider's crew, probably,' somebody said.

'Hullo! Submariners, too!'

These were the first Germans I had seen for two years, and in common with the rest of mankind I have, reprehensibly, a peculiar, unhealthy interest in gazing upon prisoners, whether civilians or those of battle. About forty men, dressed in a miscellany of clothes – blue dungarees, serge trousers, wind jackets, sweaters, brown prisoner-of-war outfits – climbed the gangway to board the tender. Many were young, a few jaunty; none seemed to have that morose, savagely despondent air so constantly recorded in newspapers or in newsreels in London cinemas. One old, bearded man, with tanned, graven face and serene eyes, seemed more like a peasant actor from Oberammergau than a prisoner of war. There was gaiety, too, in his eyes as he raised them to smile upon us on the upper deck. There was no self-consciousness in him; he smiled benignly as if bestowing benediction. Answering his smile we smiled. I wondered whether these accidents of humanity were allowed for in *King's Regulations and Admiralty Instructions*. Looking to others at my side I noticed that they also answered the old man's smile. 'Most of these merchant marine johnnies come from Hamburg and the coastal belt,' said a commander; 'Not half so Nazi as "The Party". In fact, I think Hamburg was the last of the German cities to come to heel.'

I was grateful for the excuse to picture these men as natives of that city, remembering pleasant visits I had made there before the war. How often had I seen similar seafarers in gay and shady haunts along the Reeperbahn. I remembered a lunch shared with three Germans in Frankfurt-on-Main. That summer of 1937 seemed long ago. My host had been a professor of the graphic arts, a typographical scholar of eminence; another guest had been a young German typefounder, the third a German engraver. I had mentioned that I was leaving Frankfurt that afternoon for Scandinavia, and proposed to journey via Hamburg in order to visit that city for the first time. The professor had been interested.

'Ach, Hamburg! I am, too, from Hamburg. It is beautiful, you know. You have not been there?' and he filled my glass once more with Rhineland apple juice. 'It is gay, here and there,' he said with a laugh which shook his fat body and fleshy chins. 'You must be advised not to go to the Reeperbahn, for there is no place for a young *Englander*. You are too serious for the Reeperbahn. Perhaps you come to harm,' and he winked and laughed again, his companions smiling too.

So I went north to Hamburg, put my baggage into the Graf Moltke Hotel and went out to search for the Reeperbahn. I was twenty-six, unfashionably unskilled in the ways of night-clubs, yet I came to no harm. A tall commissionaire invited me into one dive, calling to me initially in German, but, recognising me as an Englishman, changing swiftly to fluent English with an American accent. He had been a deck-hand in cargo steamers running between Hamburg and New York, he said. He had spent some time ashore, first as a dishwasher and then as a waiter in a hot-dog stand on 42nd Street. 'So I picked up the lingo. Say, why don't you come in here? They won't skin you.'

I said I was no drinking man, and, more important, no German linguist.

'We've got some nice blondes,' he countered.

I went downstairs into a dimly-lighted dance hall. Couples and groups occupied most of the tables. The couples were serious, the groups were gay, which seems to be the usual arrangement in night-clubs I have since visited in other cities. I ordered coffee and wondered whether this dreary experience could be accounted as seeing the night-life of a great port, but within a few minutes I was the sixth member of a pidgin-English party. The others were two German mercantile marine officers – a second officer and a radio engineer –and three German girls – two gay brunettes and a sombre blonde. The men had a smattering of colourful English; I had my modicum of schoolboy German. At the tables the girls spoke only with smiles, but, upon the dance floor, with the firm, comfortable hold of accomplished companions. It was a foolish and friendly spree and I was not rooked. My friends of the evening had not permitted such conventions ... and I smiled, regarding from the upper deck of a Clyde tender, the prisoners-of-war who had evoked these forgotten fragments from the years of peace.

The merchant seamen were followed by about thirty Nazi submariners, as tough a crew as any pirate could wish to collect, an assembly fully capable of 'machinations, hollowness, treachery and all ruinous disorders'. I had not seen the militant Nazi since visiting Germany in 1938; no specimen of that time could compare with the sullen arrogance of these defeated U-boat warriors, skulking aboard. Some of them carried their air of would-be toughness to such extremes that they seemed almost childish, rather like Hollywood 'dead-end' kids in their determination to look ferocious; so firmly had they been gripped by the villainous melancholy of the Nazi philosophy.

All prisoners were grouped forrard under the fo'c'sle head. There they stamped their feet or paced their minute space. The merchant seamen joked and smiled, the U-boat men brooded heavily as if scourged by the ignominy of captivity at the hands of a race of underlings.

'Not much strength-through-joy in that outfit,' said the commander.

'The old bearded gentleman seems joyful enough,' said another.

'Oh, I'm not including him. It's that U-boat crowd. What a gang to have around to Sunday night supper!'

Upon that conclusion, it seemed, the commander was prepared to rest his case. I watched them for a while and then moved across to the less depressing spectacle of the Clyde and our ship.

❧

Coming alongside the *Queen Mary* was like coming alongside a cliff and a community of cliff-dwellers, for some of the kitchen staff and hundreds of young aircraft trainees were watching our arrival from their great height. We clambered on board, following most carefully the best naval tradition in making way for senior officers, following this tradition to an unnecessary degree of courtesy in allowing a captain of Royal Marines to step upon the Monster before ourselves, a group of naval lieutenants.

The next half-hour, however, was a mockery of Service tradition and routine. Loudspeakers blared instructions in BBC, Cockney, Glaswegian and Canadian. A precise voice, addressed to 'Royal Navy personnel', directed us to the ship's office where, we were told, we should receive cabin numbers

and instructions. We forced our way through a first-night
throng to the naval office. Behind a cubby-hole, rather like a
theatre box-office, a young Wren rating ticked our names on
a typewritten list, gave us cabin numbers and then directed
us to an adjacent office, where we should receive notice of
our duties and responsibilities whilst on board. She was icy,
unapproachable. Perhaps the proximity of a RN paymaster
commander brooding over another typewritten list submitted
by a nervous Wren writer at taut attention, had this chilling
effect upon her. She was impervious to the gentle wit of
lieutenants, RN, RNR, or RNVR. Her gaze was as remote, her
voice as impersonal as a Selfridge lift girl. A RN lieutenant,
with disarming innocence, asked whether she would remain
on board to make the trip, and received the steely reply, 'Next
please!' She had no blue stripes of command about her arm,
not even that anchor or 'hook' which would have labelled
her 'Leading Wren', yet she dragooned us as if we were but
little children.

We moved along to learn our duties from a paymaster-
lieutenant, RNVR. I was given supernumerary lookout duties
on the bridge. Others, given this task, groaned aloud, for it
meant that we should have standing watches throughout
the voyage; those who had mess-deck, kitchen or gun-crew
inspections could carry out their tasks at specified times,
morning and evening, and then return to the lounge, their
drinks and their books.

I asked a steward for directions and staggered down to M
deck with my bags. Cabin 140 was already crowded. Eight
officers would occupy this narrow space. Noting the closed
scuttle, I thought that a heavy atmosphere would certainly
lull us to sleep at nights, but sudden rumour said that lunch
awaited those who were spry and I went below with another
inmate of Cabin 140.

The food was good and things seemed brighter.

During the afternoon we were given a straight-from-the-shoulder lecture by the Officer Commanding Troops. 'We are about to engage in a major operation of war. The enemy is anxious to discover our whereabouts and to destroy us. It is your duty ...' and so on. These exhortations were followed by a short, modest lecture by the Captain. We were enjoined not to smoke on deck, and not to throw waste matter overboard. We were told that we were lucky going westward, for we should have three meals a day: two meals was the routine on many passages. We must be fully acquainted with our boat stations, by day and by night, and must not move about the ship without our lifebelts. A complicated and mildly humorous demonstration of the correct manner for wearing the lifebelt was then given. It seemed impossible that anybody could ever clothe himself in the belt in less than an hour. Questions were then invited. Somebody, very brave, asked whether the ship were wet or dry. 'I imagine you mean alcoholic or non-alcoholic.' (Laughter.) 'This ship is alcoholic.' (Cheers.) 'A great deal of Coca-Cola is also drunk.' (Groans.) We were then dismissed.

We lay in the stream until the night. The liner was more than a hundred miles off the coast before I woke. During the morning we had boat drill and were given our watches. I was put in charge of one of the lifeboats, amidships, port side. My crew (if the worst were to happen) faced me: a youthful crowd of about fifty RAF trainees, some with shining morning faces; others already aware of the strange motions of the ocean.

I made a few inquiries before inspection by the OC Troops.
'Has anybody here ever done any sailing?'
Not one.
'Does anybody know anything about small boats?'
Not one.
They came, I supposed, from the inland shires, and the great cities. Few men knowing something of boats or sailing

would have been likely to be in the RAF at that stage of the war, although the most expert dinghy helmsman I had known before the war had been a regular RAF squadron-leader, a consistent winner of cups, spoons and points. I chose two strong-seeming youths as the men who would control the disengaging gear of the lifeboat, but, first, I wanted to master the working of that gear myself. I was relieved to hear, after boat drill, that one of the liner's deck officers had been assigned to demonstrate to all officers this mechanism for getting lifeboats away. I will not essay to translate his vivid instructions into the less colourful words which make this record. The gear was unusual, but simple and decisive in action, a reassuring fact, for the lifeboats were so huge that normal disengaging gear might have precipitated a grim battle for discipline against rout had the many thousands on board this liner been suddenly faced with the prospect of death by drowning. I was more attentive than usual when presented with a mechanical contrivance. I would not have wished, in a crisis, to find myself the captain of the fifty RAF trainees and to have to greet them with the confession that I had not yet mastered the correct technical background for that summons, 'Lifeboat away!' I stayed on deck, listening to the instructor, moving across the void between lifeboat deck and outswung boat trying to visualise the problems which might confront me if one U-boat commander were successful. Finally I had the drill and method fixed in my mind. Yet it could only be an imagined picture, I knew, and hoped it would be no more, for always actuality would bring events and crises never envisaged. I tried to consider every possible and impossible problem the day or night might bring, but knew that I should be a tyro again if an end should come to this ship. So I tried to learn and then put aside all brooding.

At noon I was due on the bridge. Twelve junior officers formed each watch, so that our tricks were not unbearably arduous. Day and night, six officers were spaced across the port and starboard sides of the bridge. We took one hour on, one hour off, a second hour on. On alternate watches the first hour or the last hour was always off, so that we were never called upon for more than three-hour spells of duty, and of those three hours only two were active duty. We were supposed to be within hailing distance, but this aspect of our duties was hazy, and usually we raced back to our cabins to sleep for fifty minutes. Our watch was most exact in its timekeeping, reliefs came most carefully upon their hours, but often, like that soldier of ancient Denmark, I was bitter cold and sick at heart, for we had typical Atlantic weather, great gales by day which carried vast cumulus towards the east, and sudden remorseless storms of hail by night, and we could not stir a yard from our stations.

That bridge, which curves like a vast scimitar from each side of the bridge house, thus became for a brief while a place of duty. I had seen many photographs of its great sweeping lines, for at the time of the launching of the *Queen Mary* I had, in company with many millions, been an interested reader of newspaper accounts of the miracles of marine engineering and architecture contained within the hull of this empress, greyhound, queen, etc, etc, of the seas. That bridge had been announced as one of the architectural novelties of the age, and I remember having remarked, with the pontification allowed a designer in one profession towards the designer in another, that this feature seemed to be one of the few real concessions to a twentieth-century conception of a ship, although many Elizabethan galleons and nineteenth-century tea clippers were certainly built with most graceful bridges across the full beam of the ship. I had been unmoved by most of the other rhodomontade about the *Queen Mary*. She had seemed vast, but undistinguished, rather like one of those ample old English dowagers of undoubtedly aristocratic origins but with inconspicuous aesthetic grace. From my earliest youth I had believed fervently that the best ships were also beautiful ships (as I had also innocently believed that the 'best' people were also the most beautiful!) but now, I thought, I might be persuaded to change that view as I stood upon the bridge of this great ship and assumed a pleasing shape towards the elements. She was certainly a good ship, but she was certainly not a beautiful ship.

The open bridge of the *Queen Mary*, although well designed, is no sinecure on grim nights. The captain of the liner, the officer of the watch, helmsman, signaller and runner, were enclosed within the protected bridge house, a group apart, holding no communion with us. In their eyes we were supernumeraries given a job in order that we might be kept from mischief. Sometimes they gazed briefly upon us from their comfortable house, stared again at the ocean and retreated into their shelter.

Apart from experience in ocean racing and offshore sailing I have never been a good watchkeeping subject, and my spells of duty in the *Queen Mary* were down to my usual standard. I was bored, my companions also: and it was well perhaps for the many passengers that their safety did not depend in any high degree upon our skill, keenness or delight in watchkeeping. We were told that our duties were important, that upon us fell the responsibility of watching for the wake of periscopes racing to intercept us, but I had told that tale too often to too many lookouts to make an ideal listener. We knew that we were there chiefly to keep us busy.

So we stood and stared into the seas by day and into the night by night. Often we talked amongst ourselves and frequently received word from the officer of the watch that talking was forbidden. It is certain that in this indulgence we were in grievous error, but as this is an attempt at a truthful record of a transatlantic passage under wartime conditions I record these details with an additional footnote that I cannot feel deeply conscience-stricken by this confession. We were rather like professional conjurors at a performance of the Magicians' Club. Most of us had served in small warships; most of us had urged ratings to the task of spotting U-boats, but in this great liner, crossing the ocean at a faster cruising speed than any destroyer could maintain, we doubted the purpose of our sojourn upon the bridge, yet, inevitably, of course, we all watched fairly intensively. During the bright days we stared into the seas, engrossed, as all sailors are engrossed, by wave formations, daydreamed, and were undoubtedly glad to have this inescapable reason for escaping from the enervating lounge; in times of storm we pulled on our oilskins and sou'westers and settled disconsolately to watch. At 0400 hours, however, we were in no mood to see an overwhelming need for our presence upon the bridge, and we tumbled from our bunks, cursing our reliefs, the sea, the *Queen Mary,* her captain and OC Troops.

❧

My two companions on the port side of the watch were brothers, both engineer sub-lieutenants, RNVR, and both serving in the Navy under T124 regulations, which gave them an independence denied to most other junior officers, for if they did not like a berth they could quit the Service. One brother, Paul Black, had been in the RAF as a pilot. He had served in the Middle East before the war and as a glider pilot during the war; he was tough, worldly-wise, cynical and humorous. His brother, Richard, was much younger, quite untouched by this cynicism, and equally lively in humour. They were inseparable, and were pleasant and unconventional companions for lookout duties. Paul wished always to talk, cynically; Richard, to argue, idealistically. I usually listened to their anecdotes and theories spoken fiercely against the wind's fierce breath, nodding, smiling, and looking seawards, hoping always that if the captain of the ship should see us he would account this the spirit of watchkeeping if not the letter. Twice he sent out word that these were misplaced hopes.

During the day, when we were not upon the bridge or at boat stations, we were in the great, gutted lounge of the liner. There we read, played draughts, chess, backgammon, poker or whist. A dozen women were on board – three Canadian nurses, two ATS, four young mothers and three smart young women difficult to label – and they were subjected to pursuit by the several dozen Lotharios on board. Most of the women seemed to enjoy the experience, and it was amusing to note how fully capable they were of drinking nip for nip with Canadian or British naval and army officers and Big Businessmen from Birmingham, Warwickshire, or Birmingham, Alabama.

Even in peacetime, life in the lounges of great liners is often boring; the restrictions of war made this boredom in the Monster even more emphatic. Drink brought escape from boredom for many travellers, but the price was heavy, to judge by the long-faced creatures who peered wanly at the splendid breakfasts and then drank only blackest coffee. (Later in the war I travelled once more in the Monster and drink was denied all such escapees, unless they had been forewarned and had illegally brought drink on board. This decision to make the ship wholly 'dry' seemed to be wise, for I have heard the views of the lower-deck upon that honoured naval tradition whereby officers may drink their gins and whiskeys from Saccone and Speed and no drink may be consumed on board by ratings. Such distinctions have done much to foster 'pigs aft' as the normal reference to the wardrooms of big ships. Rumour said that American influence made British troopships 'dry' at that later stage in the war: but I never learned the truth. The advantages, however, were obvious, and, strangely enough, were acknowledged by men who sipped at Coca-Colas when their palates craved harsher satisfaction.)

Others escaped by reading or by playing marathon bridge. In the five days of the voyage I read through the first volume of *War and Peace*, a pleasure which, I have been told, takes a month in the normal life of a lawkeeping citizen. The princes Bolkonsky and Hippolyte, Anna Mikhaylovna, Count Nikolai Rostov, and that concourse of Russian aristocrats became my companions through the hours and days. I think that this intensive approach is perhaps the most satisfactory manner of reading Tolstoy's book. The early chapters slip more easily into their true significance as an introduction to a fabulous story, do not become a wearisome means of assembling a vast, unwieldy cast, as so many would-be readers assert. To those who must meet these strange creatures with their complicated names whilst moving between train and office and home, those early chapters must be a strain. Once again I thought that those who journeyed to and from the war had more pleasant times than those who must stay at home or journey to and from a desk or lathe.

We spent scant time in our cabins and then only to sleep or to wash or to bath in hot salt water which gushed from the taps with the wildness of Lodore. Sometimes in the afternoons we slept, but this is a habit of professional seamen and one I have never fully mastered. Yet even during the scant hours we spent in our cabin our knowledge of each other's lives became wider if not deeper.

Usually we talked of the Service and of our pre-war jobs and of the jobs to which we journeyed. Inevitably, sometimes in bitterness, usually in nostalgia, details of civilian life came into our recitals of war.

Three of the eight lieutenants in the cabin were RNR. They professed to loathe the sea which had, for so many years, given them their earnings. They longed always to escape to dry land and to jobs ashore. They were grimmer in their appraisal of the way of life of a sailor, more sceptical, more serious than ourselves. They could not consider any other way of life although they might dream of other jobs; their training would keep them to the sea. They wished to rebel but no technique of rebellion had grown within them. They termed us, RNVR, lucky, saying that we had jobs awaiting our return, but two Fleet Air Arm youngsters smiled and damned this prospect for themselves. 'I was up at Cambridge when it started,' said an observer; 'I was twenty-one. I stayed up another year to take my degree and now I'm twenty-four. If the war lasts another four years – and it will – I shall be nearly thirty. I shall have a pass degree in history and not a day's solid work to my credit. If I live and if I'm lucky I shall be a teacher in a secondary school in the provinces. I may like that, but even if I don't I shall be too old to change. So what?' The other, continuing, said: 'I'm twenty-one. I'd just left school when this show started. If the war does last all the time that Freeman says, I shall be twenty-five and not even a pass degree to call my own. I shall have a pilot's certificate and a hundred thousand other chaps will have the same. If I'm very lucky I may be a civil air pilot. I quite like flying. If I'm moderately lucky I shall be a car dealer in Great Portland Street. If I'm unlucky I shall be on the bare bones of my backside.'

'What did you hope to be?' I asked.

'I wanted to be a doctor,' he said.

'Couldn't you have been reserved for that?'

'I could have been. My old man's a doctor and he wanted to get me reserved, but I rushed off and joined up, and told him afterwards. Was he mad!'

I asked whether he had regrets.

'Not about that,' he said. 'Actually, I really do like flying. Who wouldn't? But I do have regrets about the future, if you see what I mean. I suppose they'll keep a lot of chaps in the Service, but they won't want all of us. I suppose it'll all work out in the end. I've had a good war and I've been jolly lucky. Had two crashes and I'm still here. Can't really grumble. I suppose I ought really to consider myself well-off with accelerated promotion – two stripes and all that, but I sometimes get depressed.'

'I still think you're lucky,' said a RNR officer, about forty. 'You've at least got the youth and energy to leave the sea. I haven't even got that. It's the only life I know. It wasn't all beer and skittles before the war and by the time the Yanks have finished this damned great fleet of Liberty ships, it'll be a sight worse peace than it is war – at least for us.'

There were six of us in the cabin. We leaned against the bunks which had been built with efficient economy throughout the ship. Another of the RNR officers opened his suitcase to take out a shirt. A large photograph of a woman and child was pasted firmly inside the lid; it was easy to guess his reasons for wishing to leave the sea. The other two occupants of the cabin came in just before lunch. We continued to talk of the prospects of the distant peace and its effect upon seafarers. The professional seamen were jocular in bitter suspicion of the Government.

'We were forgotten before and we'll be forgotten again,' one said.

'Before I'm fifty I shall be glad to ship for a deckhand's berth,' said another: and against this realistic pessimism we, representatives of the junior, unprofessional reserve of the Royal Navy, could place no words of reassurance or of hope.

We broke from such depression to talk about the craft we were to join. Two of us were going to corvettes; two to cruisers under repair in Brooklyn Navy Yard; one RNR lieutenant to a Woolworth carrier being converted from a mercantile hull in San Francisco; the other was rejoining, after compassionate leave in England, his destroyer, undergoing repairs in Newport. The two airmen were proceeding to the Fleet Air Arm station in Trinidad. Ages ranged from the twenty-one years of the pilot to the forty-odd years of one of the RNR officers.

Interests and hobbies probably varied more widely than age. In conversation our common interest in the Service and the ships in which we served made us unadventurous. In humour we engaged a native zest for ribaldry and a mockery of a tradition which we all undoubtedly respected. In outlook we were avowedly pessimists but incurably optimists.

❧

Each warship in the fleet has its daily 'buzz'. 'Tonight we shall up anchor and leave for Murmansk,' says rumour at eight bells: or 'The old man is giving shore leave this afternoon, two hours each watch': or 'The Hun has a new mine that goes up when an aeroplane passes within two miles. U-boats are laying 'em in hundreds. Can't be attacked by Coastal Command. See?' and so on and so on.

The Monster too had its many buzzes. 'Ernie Bevin's on board. Going over to tell the Yanks how to get their women into uniform': or 'Did you hear we were rerouted six times yesterday? Had a wolf pack dead ahead': or 'We are to rendezvous with five destroyers a thousand miles off New York. They nearly lost this old tub last trip': or 'All the

Czechoslovak gold in Britain's on board': and so on and so on. The daily buzz was always novel, always entertaining, always inaccurate.

In conversation and with more accurate results, we learned of others on board. We talked to each other and about each other. On the second day out one of the Fleet Air Arm pilots said: 'You're going to a corvette, aren't you?'

I agreed.

'As Number One?'

Again I agreed.

'Know her name?' Hearing *Tobias* he said: 'I think your Old Man's over there. I was talking to him this morning and that's the name of the ship he's going to as CO. Said he thought his Jimmy might be on board.'

I looked across the lounge. A group of naval and RAF officers had formed a lively drinking school. I asked my oracle which of the school I should begin to respect.

'That dark, sullen-looking bloke. Two-and-a-half-striper, RNVR.' I had thought, with my first glance to the group, that this was probably the man, and asked his name.

'Willoughby. Actually, he seems quite a decent chap. Shouldn't go by his face too much. Looks a bit gloomy at the moment, I must admit. Probably being with those RAF types. Enough to get anyone down. Always yapping about the number of times they circled the target and all that.'

The sailor with wings seemed professionally piqued about something, but I was too anxious to know more about my Captain to inquire. The 'decent chap' looked to us, rose and walked across the lounge. 'I hear you may be my Number One,' he said. 'No, don't get up. May I join you?' and he took a chair by the small table. In this way I met my Captain. He bought me a Coca-Cola and himself a gin. Later I returned this gesture, and through the afternoon, until my watch at five o'clock, we talked together.

Mainly we talked about corvettes. This was Willoughby's first command. I gathered that he had been in a Tribal class destroyer in the Norwegian campaign, and had then been drafted as First Lieutenant to one of the earlier corvettes. Now he would get his chance as a Commanding Officer.

'Will you enjoy that?' I asked.

'I think so. It'll certainly be less arduous a job than a Jimmy's as you'll find out for yourself fairly soon', and he smiled, somewhat queerly. I had known this to be a true estimate of a First Lieutenant's job in most of the smaller service ships and was not shocked by the news. Willoughby asked many questions. What experience had I gained before the war? Did I get sick in corvettes? Did I like corvettes? Was I any good at navigation? Or gunnery? Or the asdic? Occasionally he stayed his questioning to place his own views under examination. I liked his apparent tolerance and lack of pomposity. He seemed natural in manner, grave in purpose and gay in announcing that purpose. It was easy to see that his personality was strong, but not strong in wilfulness or dogmatism; rather in maturity and balance. My luck with my Captains still held, I told myself later on the bridge, but tried not to be too optimistic.

❧

We talked each day, chiefly shop, but also of other things; our peacetime lives, books, films, plays, sport and the half-dozen other subjects which enter into the conversations of middle-class Englishmen. Usually we met in the mornings or afternoons. In the evenings Willoughby concentrated on bridge or poker, for he was, he confessed, a consistent gambler, and the wardroom of *Tobias* would soon become a gambling hell if he got half a chance. Perhaps it was as well that I was no card-player. In this way we began to learn the edge of each other's character. My first impressions remained. He was serious, but with sudden releases from seriousness. Usually these releases were in conversational tangents, but I thought that once away from the confines of the ship he might well be capable of other less innocent tangential escapes.

～❧

We had been re-routed twice, a deck officer said, and as we travelled far to the south the nearer sun gave credence to wild words of rumour. Then the Monster turned again to the north and winds and storms came once more into our lives. We longed for shore.

'Tomorrow we shall be there,' said Paul Black. 'Probably in our early morning watch we shall see the old Nantucket tub', and at three o'clock in the morning a stabbing flicker of light at the world's rim held our eyes. 'The Ambrose light,' said Paul authoritatively. Word came from the Captain: his compliments and we were now released from further watchkeeping duties: would we kindly inform our reliefs? I stayed on the bridge for another ten minutes, watching the distant light. Tomorrow I would be in New York. I was quite excited and hoped against hope that I should get a chance to explore.

Breakfast was a gay, scamped meal. Even the mariners of the *Santa Anna* could have known no keener excitement in their landfall. We moved quickly from the dining rooms to watch the tugs edge us to our berth. I stood by the rail, wishful to be alone. The skyline of Manhattan, the ceaseless ferries, the tugs and liners, tankers and coasters, gave to the early morning a magic I had not known for several years. I was as unencumbered with reservations upon delight as I had been on my first journey abroad, to Scandinavia ten years before. I could not bear to think that I should miss one moment of this time. The Hudson and its vast piers were as thrilling as the quieter timbered wharves of Haugesund, skyscrapers were as beautiful as the Town Hall tower of Stockholm. So deeply coloured and susceptible is imagination at these times.

Commuters, travelling to their New York desks, waved from the ferries. Beyond them, beyond the piers, were the great warehouses and stores. Beyond these buildings were the beginnings of the great city with that skyline so often seen in films yet scarcely ever credible to anyone from Europe. Even the greyness of this day and of this city brought no depression. The air was sharp, exhilarating. I recalled passages from Corbusier's book on New York. Even he, the sophisticated architect and visionary, had been dazzled and enthralled by the fantastic city. I wished for a moment that I had brought with me his little-known book, *Quand les Cathédrales étaient blanches.* Corbusier's swift nervous line drawings seem to recapture this skyline more truthfully, more imaginatively, than the inevitable photographic shots of towering Rockefeller Centres and Chrysler Buildings pricking at the clouds.

∾

Five and a half days after leaving the Clyde we docked at the Cunard Pier. We spent three hours watching our entry to the New World. I wished to be ashore. I wished also to watch. Over-ruling all lesser wishes, however, was my desire to get at least two days in New York. Perhaps, like more ancient, more purposeful mariners, I should have been more wishful to rush headlong to Halifax and thence to the Atlantic Battle, but I was now as sceptical of such haste as a professional seaman. My presence will not speed the building of the ship by five fewer minutes I said suavely and convincingly to a quiescent conscience. Willoughby, standing at the rail a few paces off, called: 'Do you know this town?'

I shook my head.

'Worth knowing. We must see that we miss a few trains to Halifax. I've one or two dates which may still be open.' At noon we were told we should leave the ship. All naval officers would form a group at the ship's office and proceed ashore to a waiting coach. We stood around, wondering what New York girls would be like (that unceasing, never-answered query, with never a realist to say that they could scarcely be like Chinese girls or scarcely unlike American girls): what American food would be like, what everything American would be like. For most of us this was to be an introduction to The New World: I saw few signs of that so-called British reserve in the party of naval officers waiting to go ashore. In fact, we were as excited as a girls' school crocodile.

❧

The Barbizon-Plaza Hotel on 6th Avenue and 58th Street is likely to become one of the legends of the Royal Navy in its second World War. Thousands of British naval officers stayed in that comfortable skyscraper hotel. For most of them the Barbizon-Plaza was introduction to New York life. Many remained for one night and then moved on across the continent to the Pacific Coast, or south to the ports of the Caribbean or north to Canada. Others, appointed to ships building, converting or refitting in Brooklyn Navy Yard, remained in the Barbizon-Plaza for weeks and sometimes months. These we accounted the luckier warriors in the Atlantic Battle.

Within the hotel, a RN routine seemed to be well-established. We were given brief instructions and an advance of thirty dollars from our PLA – provision and lodging allowance. Afterwards I saw Willoughby in the lounge. He smiled with undisguised delight.

'I'm happy to tell you, Number One, that in the best British tradition nobody expected us, nobody knows anything about us, nobody's even heard of our ship. I suppose somebody at the Navy Yard does. I'll find out this afternoon. Meantime, let's have lunch. I'll wander over to the Senior Naval Officer later. You ought to look around.' We lunched at a small restaurant, The Hamburger Inn, on 57th Street, a small place with black girls as waitresses and a rich repertory of simple food – if Maryland chicken and lemon pies could be termed 'simple food' by an Englishman fresh from British wartime fare. This lunch began four days of wholehearted holiday in New York. For me they were four of the swiftest days of my life. I saw no Englishmen, apart from Willoughby at lunch, but spent my days alone or with American friends not seen since days of peace in London. This book can hold but little space for remembering these times, for during these days I was no longer an amateur sailor but another English visitor gaining his first experience of American hospitality.

I made slight and sober acquaintance with New York Cafe Society; listened to Hildegarde singing at the Savoy Plaza; explored Central Park, Harlem, Broadway; visited friends in apartments and studios on the 'east-fifties'; watched forgotten French and Russian film classics at the Museum of Modern Art; saw *Porgy and Bess* on Broadway, listening excitedly to Gershwin's melodies; went to Schrafts for five o'clock English teas (an only concession to a native background); journeyed often to no particular places by the 'el' and by subway; bought silk stockings at Macys, face powder at Saks and nylon brassières at Lord and Taylor (and lest these seem strange purchases for a sailor I hasten to add that they were packed for shipment to feminine names in English homes by young American salesgirls and I continued on my New York wanderings without embarrassment); I rubber-necked in Wall Street, Washington Square, Battery Place and Greenwich

Village. I 'did' a hundred places in my hundred hours; I was as zestful and as energetic as any American sightseer at the Louvre, upon Tower Hill or by St Peter's. I was the unashamed tourist in an unashamed city.

Always New Yorkers were insistently keen to know about the war across the ocean. Thoughts and memories of Dunkirk had remained in their minds with strange constancy, and nobody would believe that I was more keen to know how many negroes lived in New York than I was to talk about the war at sea. 'More British understatement,' they said, and I could only shake my head in despair, assuring them that I liked New York too much to wish to return immediately to the Europe to which I must, alas, return soon enough.

I had no time for sociological inquiry. I knew that many New Yorkers lived in wickedly cramped quarters. I was not involved with problems of the rights and wrongs of the war. These things I would leave for more earnest travellers. I merely moved and stared, and slept for fewer hours than I had ever slept within a similar span of days and nights at sea.

Not all Englishmen were so pleasantly occupied in and with New York. To many it was an unfriendly place and they talked narrowly of its people and its show places as many Americans talked, at a later date, of Londoners and their monuments. These, however, were sad creatures, expectant that New York should come out to find them, unused to new places, others' ways of thought, unadventurous within their minds and upon their feet. For most of us New York became for a brief, free spell a place of gaiety and delight, friendliness and warmth, and always unending generosity. I think most British sailors would share these views. It is certain that the brothers Black shared them, for they became immediately involved in passionately-conducted friendships with two sisters who lived out at Scarsdale and came daily into New York in the family's second car, a great Buick cabriolet, in order that the two brothers might be shown Long Island scenery in a civilised manner. At the weekend all four would travel up to Vermont, where the family had a farm run on strictly scientific principles, 'and as I was trained as a scientist, Eleanor thinks I ought to give the farm the once over,' said Paul, unctuously.

They were both lucky, they claimed, for their ship was at the Brooklyn Navy Yard and the engine-room was not yet ready for examination. 'In fact, there's not even a boiler room yet,' said Paul.

'The old man says we'd better take ten days' leave. So here we are. Who can blame us?' Certainly not I, was my sad admission, for Willoughby and myself were to leave the following morning for Halifax and I was loth to go.

~&~

We travelled towards *Tobias*, slowly up through New England into the Maritime Provinces, thence to Nova Scotia. It was a long but pleasant journey. I moved steadily through the second volume of *War and Peace* and read, as relief, I remember, two *Modern Library* books, *Seven Gothic Tales* and *Java Head*. Willoughby sat opposite reading the first volume of *War and Peace*. Through the days we read, ate, slept, gazed from the windows, and I wrote letters. The late spring sun lazed blandly upon great spans of farmland; farmers moved between their painted clapboard homes and widespread fields with the unhurried steps of farmers in all the world. Sometimes our train stopped in the middle of the high streets of small towns. We descended and stepped into scenes which we had seen often enough in films but thought never to see in life. In such homespun, ten-gallon-hat communities our naval uniforms were incongruous, conspicuous, and we were immediately drawn into lively answers to livelier questions until the long-drawn, echoing 'All aboard!' from the black guards took us once more back to our seats and books. We spent two nights and almost two days in the train. It was a journey we wished to continue for many days. There was no boredom in the many miles, but only continuing novelty in watching Americans and Canadians in their own rich lands.

Chapter 3
The Building of *Tobias*

Two mornings later we inspected HMS *Tobias*. She was not impressive, being no more than a hull, and even thus a hull fashioned in new-fangled ways: by welder and burner and not by a stabbing swarm of riveters. We picked a way across the dingy shipyard and there was our ship, indistinguishable from three other hulls in adjoining slipways. She carried no sign of individuality, no touch of distinctive quality. She was the nondescript hull of a nondescript warship and I thought of youthful days in boatbuilding yards where even two yachts of the same class begin to show their individuality in the first weeks of their building. Of four hulls any one might have been *Tobias*. 'She's certainly no beauty,' said the Captain as we came away that afternoon, and that was our verdict upon our ship.

❧

The Chief Engineer was already in the yard. He had been in attendance for three weeks. 'Not that I've made much difference,' he said to the Captain. 'Only the noo they've started to think about yon engine-room, sir, but ye ken it's guid to have somebody aboot.'

'I think so, too, Chief,' said the Captain. 'D'you like Halifax?'

The Chief thought he did; people were kind, he said, and the food wonderful, especially after a base job in Freetown since the beginning of the war, but the town landladies were 'bitches oot for every penny piece'. Dundass was a Warrant Officer, doubtless given warrant rank at the outbreak of war and now sent to us for sea time. He was a short, burly Scot, with sandy hair, red face, enormous chin and broad vowels. He carried within himself a self-confidence and a sense of quick understanding of the tasks about and ahead of him that I found reassuring; I suspected that Willoughby, too, found relief in the meeting, for much would depend upon the engine-room and particularly its overseer.

'Would ye like t'meet the foreman, sir?' asked Dundass.

'I think not, not at this stage,' said the Captain. 'You seem to be doing very well and he might start on technicalities.'

Dundass smiled, understanding. His jaw jutted; white teeth sundered his red face in appreciation of the joke and compliment. This was Willoughby's way, I thought. From the beginning he would have Dundass on his side.

We walked away. 'Useful type, I imagine,' said the Captain. 'Useful, too, to have the Chief as a member of the wardroom. So much shop can be talked and learned in the wardroom atmosphere of tobacco and gin.'

We walked along the ship, trying to think how it was possible that this hulk, shaping but lifeless, would take us to the Atlantic within a month, or so the builders claimed. 'I cannot see it,' said the Captain, 'yet I suppose they'll do it.'

❧

In this way we began our watch upon *Tobias*. Inevitably in those days of building, Willoughby and myself were together for much of our time, and were, in fact, scarcely ever separated for more than an hour or so. Our personalities did not grate, and our friendship began.

We spent the days in a recurring routine, rising from our camp-beds in the overcrowded boarding-house at six o'clock, throwing on our clothes, stumbling down the uncarpeted stairs and into a street car. The car took us about a mile and then we transferred to the shipbuilding company's lorry, which took some of the workers to the yard. 'Thank God,' said Willoughby more than once, 'this pantomime will be over as soon as we can get the cabins or the wardroom almost straight. We can doss down there,' and I agreed, for this commuting to and from the ship seemed an undignified and comic progress to a ship.

At the yard we gulped down hot coffee at the canteen, and by a quarter-to-eight were once more climbing about the shaping ship, talking to carpenters, welders, electricians, engineers and the score of other foremen to whom this was another job of work, and not their home and destiny for future days. Little wonder if they sometimes thought us pernickety in the way we talked about minute points of ventilation and heating, or discussed the galley arrangements with the air of Alexis Soyer himself! This supervision, often amateurish on our part, continued until eleven, when we went for more coffee and, invariably, a slice of apple pie. After that indulgence we were usually caught into dozens of small conferences: about the deck, upon the bridge, on the gun platforms or the quayside or below decks; sometimes even upon the high pinnacles of the travelling crane! At other times we were drawn into blue-print discussions in the engine-room, but not often. Willoughby was at pains to avoid these engine-room discussions. Again he made his philosophy quite clear.

'They're your job, Chief!' he said. 'Come to me by all means if you want an argument backed up by any bluff or bullying I can provide, but don't land me in any technical discussion, or my ignorance will be all round Halifax in a couple of hours. You know I know nothing about turbines, so do I, but I don't want this shipbuilding yard and the rest of Halifax to know.' The Chief smiled, his great jaw out-thrust with his monstrous grin. 'It'll only be a wee bit o' high-handed patter I'll mebbe wantin' ye for, sir. I'm not so guid at that meself. I talk their own language and that's a beeg meestake!' 'I think you've a profound truth there, Chief,' said Willoughby, edging away to the inspection of riveters at the base of a gun platform. 'What about lunch, Number One?' The mere fact that he had heard *Tobias* carried quadruple-expansion reciprocating engines was enough to terrify the First Lieutenant, who had never even known how to take his first scooter to pieces. We went quickly to lunch.

❧

Much of my own supervision was concerned with mess-deck accommodation. Whilst in *Solander* I had been in the crew's quarters only about half a dozen times, and thus had but slight knowledge of the views of the seamen concerning a corvette's quarters. I knew that they were considered almost adequate and reasonable, but I was anxious to include those modest additions which might ease the harshness of life in the lower-deck. This was not indulgence but sanity. Ancient days of weevil-ridden biscuits and sea-soaked sacking were gone, and although touchy old gentlemen in clubs might contend that the perilous state of the Empire in 1939 had been due to the discarding of these customs, I could not agree. I had my own experience in the trawler *Alaskan* to call upon, and I had no wish to duplicate in *Tobias* the living conditions of that sturdy ship, for I remembered too vividly the return from Norway, with half our freeboard missing and the wounded on board.

I had found transition from civilian life to the lower-deck emphatic and salutary, and I knew that half of the crew of *Tobias* (now somewhere on the Atlantic on their way to join us) would be almost civilians, for their few weeks' shore training at Chatham, Portsmouth, Sheerness or some other base had merely clothed them in the semblance of seamen and could scarcely have made them even very ordinary seamen. I remembered how personal idiosyncrasies and fads became enlarged, and personal fastidiousness a joke in the communal life of a minor vessel of war. That I had seen in *Alaskan* when bad weather caught us, and sickness seized two of the men, suddenly, mercilessly. Their retching had taken them tottering to 'the heads'. They had returned, fallen into their bunks and were sick again, their mess sweeping their bunks and the decks. I smiled, recalling how I had kept to my bunk, jamming myself against its iron edge, trying to read, my stomach reacting dismally to the nausea of others, my eyes drawn irresistibly to their wretchedness. Later, a man, bold in bravado, had opened a tin of fruit salad, taken his fill and then swiftly vomited across his blankets. It was an extreme folly, and Dick Ives had been moved to anger, cursing him for a hog and a fool, but the man, lost to shame in sickness, had collapsed in his bunk. A sorry gang of men had stirred to take the middle watch that night. Through years of sailing, my stomach, although often tortured, had never been defeated by the elements, and I was certain that it would not plunge me into what I occasionally considered the ignominy of sickness, but I was less than sure of its strength against the follies and disabilities of shipmates. These ills are more apparent in mess-decks than in cabins. Seas get below despite strong fo'c'sle-heads or bulkheads and the fierce battening of hatches. The continuing swish of waters beneath the bunks is a disturbing sound. Socks fall upon the deck, however carefully one stows them in bunk or locker. Gumboots fall upon their sides and fill with water. Trousers get soaked and press dankly upon one's legs. Shirts are sodden. Duffel coats are soggy sacks. Life is a mean existence at such times; morale falls swiftly like an ominous barometer, and men move in a stupor of resentment.

Extroverts swear savagely and thus perhaps clear their minds, but I had not this escape and consequently moved always quietly and dully to my station, appreciating the irony of contrast between such a way of life and my earlier existence, but unable to see a moral in the irony; failing, too, as usual, to see that these trials of the body might bring enhanced spiritual strength, as the philosophers assert. Like most mortals reared in tolerable comfort I hate discomfort, dirt and darkness in my living quarters. Again and again I told myself that I had experienced these conditions in yachts, but then they had been amusing. One would leave such things at the end of the race and return to hot baths and mixed grills within an hour, but in a small warship hot baths are far away, and instead of mixed grills is only lower-deck 'spudoosh', that dismal diet of many-eyed potatoes mashed with corned beef into a mockery of a meal, and always (for me) undrinkable tea.

Yet no sailor contains these despondencies for long; 'the fit is momentary, upon a thought he will again be well', and I was no exception to this rule, yet the memories of depressions came back and were goads to see that, if possible, HMS *Tobias* should not hold too many breaches for the sea and the discomforts of the sea. Thus I was careful about ventilation, heating, lighting, and all arrangements for the movement of food from the galleys to the men's quarters, particularly as such movement might be affected by bad weather. The Petty Officers would, I knew, be able to fend for themselves, for scrounging, and the ability to make themselves comfortable in their own mess, came with their years and training; but I was concerned about the forty-odd men who would come direct from civil life. Some might call such considerations mollycoddling; unrepentantly I called them realism. The more men who could accept the life, the more men *Tobias* would have on watch, and that seemed to me a rational outlook. Willoughby sometimes smiled at my preoccupation with the placing of lighting and heating points. One afternoon he said: 'Good job the crew can't see you at that job, Number One; they'd think you thought them a lot of sissies. Still they won't have much to grumble about when they do shake down. Cut out any "sea lawyer" stuff, anyway!'; and that, I knew, was his own realistic approach to the same problem.

≈

We lunched in the vast canteen-cafeteria run by the shipyard. Initially it was a terrifying experience to be caught into chattering crowds of workers, carried along in the stream, past the tables and the cafeteria benches on which were displayed immense quantities and varieties of food, even more staggering to old world eyes than New York's wartime provender, but, having, like most non-smokers, a sweet tooth, I quickly accepted the profusion and became an expert in selection from the varied pies. Willoughby was not much slower in appreciation, although he affected to despise such display as weakness in a civilised palate, reared and developed in The Ivy, the Etoile, and Boulestin's.

On the third day we were translated to an upper restaurant reserved for the directors and administrative staff of the yards. Somebody had seen Willoughby and myself engulfed in the normal milling of the canteen and had quickly invited us into what was apparently considered the rightful lunching background for officers of ships building in the yard. 'As a democrat,' said Willoughby, 'I ought to make a stand on fundamental principles and eat with the workers of the world; as a somewhat weary temporary gentleman I'm prepared to accept everything that's offered in the way of service.' We did, and thereafter were able to select our salads and pies at leisure, and watched them being brought to the table by smart young waitresses. Officers from other corvettes were there, most of them RCNVR – Royal Canadian Naval Volunteer Reserve – and within three days we were exchanging jokes, anecdotes, and details concerning building progress upon our respective craft. Most of these Canadian reserve officers were peacetime yachtsmen from the Great Lakes and many had received part of their training at *King Alfred*. A few had served in Royal Navy destroyers, but all were keen to get into their own Royal Canadian Navy, of which they were extremely proud. One said that soon the Canadian yards would be turning out Tribal class destroyers. That would be the day, when the first Canadian Tribal was commissioned! Already a flotilla was planned, and others would follow. Willoughby interested them, having served in Tribals. All implied that they would be content to serve as commanding officers, first lieutenants and junior officers in the increasing fleet of Canadian corvettes, but that destroyers, and particularly Tribals, were their ultimate ambition.

'Personally,' said Willoughby afterwards, walking back to the ship, 'they can have their Tribals. Give me *Tobias,* or, at least, give me *Tobias* if this shipyard ever gives her to me!'

The Canadians ate vast lunches, drank milk copiously, and in the evenings were gay, 'inclined to be carefree', in Willoughby's words. They helped us to make swift, correct approaches to the officials of the base and the yard. They were always kind, hospitable and lively. Sometimes they spoke of England. The food and weather of that nation they deprecated in scathing words, but some had married English girls and admitted to a desire to return to England – but only to bring their wives back to Canada, they added. Mainly, however, their words were in praise of the England that stood alone against the German bully. We were never able to evolve appropriate sentences which would turn aside these comments. We might feel slightly self-conscious, being implicated by birth in these tributes, but they were good to hear. Even the cynical Willoughby was inclined to look self-satisfied at such moments, as I pointed out, but blandly he dis agreed, terming his complacence, 'Dominions diplomacy', his own answer to 'dollar diplomacy'.

The afternoons continued in the manner of the mornings. I attended frequent impromptu conferences and made attempts to give some sort of order to the growing piles of books and signals which appeared in the half-completed wardroom, despite our efforts to take nothing on board until we were in some state of preparedness for storing and filing, but such nightmares are inseparable from the building of a ship. All relevant plans and parts cannot be dovetailed, for it is not always possible to arrange that radio equipment should arrive after the wireless cabin is ready to receive such gear; it is not always possible to stay the delivery of all stores which will not be needed for another month. We did our best. Our compromises, we knew, were being paralleled in hundreds of yards throughout the allied countries: in the Clyde, in Brooklyn, in Sydney, even in India. In all yards there will always be this seeming chaos and in all yards, presumably, most things get sorted out, and with this outlook we comforted ourselves.

In the evenings we were leisurely. Halifax was bleak, although it did its best to cope with the sudden boom thrust upon it by the war and from the sea. The town itself was like a mixture of the slums of the English north-east coast and the more prosperous middle-class homes of Bradford. We spent most of our evenings in the cinemas, of which there was providentially a profusion in the town. Our evening meals were eaten in one of the two more pretentious restaurants. These were the Normandie and the Green Lantern, and both were filled night after night with Royal Navy and Merchant Navy officers, Canadian Army officers, ATS officers and a few Wrens; other ranks also arrived in mass. There seemed to be high competition for the attentions of the few personable females; this competitive spirit seemed to brood heavily upon certain tables, fostering tension and keen words between the warring males, but those responsible seemed to enjoy this concentration of emotion, and we often smiled, watching the watching eyes of men and women.

The food was superb, and always we sat down at our tables promising ourselves these pleasures which we knew were certain to be listed on the menu: mushrooms, bacon, eggs, vanilla cream pie, coffee and cream. These, said Willoughby, were the rewards of long and faithful service to Their Lordships of the Admiralty, and he ordered a second slice of pie, but this time a variant, perhaps lemon, perhaps pumpkin. So quickly had he become a pie-addict, forgetful of earlier scoffing words concerning my greed. Now he chose authoritatively from lemon meringue, raisin, bilberry, apple, and searched for others lest some should remain untasted before our spell ashore should end and we should return to the limitations of a seagoing galley and the care of a seagoing cook.

❧

During that week *Tobias* left the slipway, moved down into the river and was slowly edged into position alongside the quays. There she would be fitted out. Now we saw only her solid, unliving hull. Perhaps the scant super-structure might help to take the title, warship, but even this we deemed deception.

⁓

Along the haphazard streets of the port, yellow street-cars clanged assertively. The colours of the cars ranged from dirty yellows, which would have been inspiration to Parisian *couturiers*, to the brighter yellows of recently painted cars. The cars gave gaiety to drab streets, and we agreed that we would willingly have viewed these colours about the streets of London and its suburbs if we had not the fierce, homely reds of our own buses. In the streets, old wooden frame houses, carelessly painted in greys, mauves and fawns, were the immediate neighbours of beauty parlours and dress shops, bright with the chromium of contemporary facades. Gas-holders, huge and grey, loomed over the lower end of the town, adjacent to the headquarters of the tramways; the composition of these sombre shapes and the yellow street-cars, enclosed within a rickety yellow fence, was a delight to the eyes, having the attraction of nineteenth-century primitives in the manner of the douanier Rousseau.

These primitive touches were evident throughout the town; houses, shops, streets and wharves seemed to have been drawn with uncouth outlines by untutored hands, then coloured with exuberant primaries alternating with sober greys and blues. I wished often that I had been a painter and not a designer, restricted to the disciplines of line, unversed in the freer world of colour. There were so many scenes to be recorded for an England used to more picturesque renderings of North Sea ports and Cornish fishing villages, yet I easily put aside these yearnings, for now I was not even a designer. The tense had changed. I *had been* a designer, but was now no more than a masquerading sailor, and that the masquerade was not perennially unmasked was my perennial surprise.

I was never allowed too long for these daydreams, for Willoughby, restless and contained within the confines of Halifax 'Cafe Society', seemed always to meditate upon grandiose schemes for escape from Nova Scotia. Once he decided we ought to fly out with Coastal Command; another time he decided that we should go to New York; a third time he wished to crew with the Grand Banks fishing fleets. He mentioned the possibility of his New York venture on our fourth night ashore. We were moving steadily through a five-course dinner in the Green Lantern. Would it not be a pleasant project, he said, for us to fly to La Guardia airfield? We could be there in five hours; all this squalor need not return into our lives for forty-eight hours; and he waved his arm airily but comprehensively around, including the pleasant restaurant, the town and seemingly all the maritime provinces. I agreed that the project sounded perfect. Then why not do it? asked Willoughby. I mentioned the permission of the authorities. Willoughby dismissed them. I asked whether he could or would leave the ship for three days at this stage in its building. Of course, he said. Then, to try him, I said that we ought to get permission the following morning. We discussed the chances. Willoughby said 100 per cent favourable, and on those odds we slept. He got permission for thirty-six hours' absence and then said we ought not to go. I had put no faith in the chances of our trip and was not dismayed when Willoughby unashamedly said that no self-respecting captain would leave his ship at such a stage. I had been chiefly interested to see how he would emerge from this sudden whim, and thought I was beginning to understand him. He would engage upon such a venture as if challenging himself. He had gained permission from the base for two days' leave, and then his basic commonsense had rejected the idea. He compromised by taking two afternoons off to play golf with a retired Canadian colonel. I spent the afternoons being motored by the Colonel's wife over a wide area of Nova Scotia. Relaxed, we returned to the task of tending HMS *Tobias* through trying weeks.

In these ways, in talking and listening through the evenings, over dinner, walking back to our dismal bedroom, I came to know something of Willoughby. There remained facets of knowledge yet to be cut by experience, but those which were apparent carried strange lights, I sometimes thought.

He was about thirty-five, unmarried and free from any sort of current emotional attachment. In appearance he was tall, just under six feet, dark, almost swarthy, and heavy featured. His eyes seemed always fierce as if he were in perpetual spleen. His movements were determined and vigorous. He was almost handsome, although his features were too irregular and too heavy for conventional good looks. Always women looked at him a second time, but he seemed unaware of their glances. His personality was strong, and to the impressionable, might prove overpowering. It would be interesting, I thought, to watch the effect of such strength upon the two officers about to join the ship. If their personalities were less than strong he would carry them along with him by the vitality of his opinions, boldly and vividly expressed. If they were equally strong there would be clashes. His wit was sardonic and seemingly inexhaustible, due probably to abounding good health. His mind was complex, given to caprice as in the project of our New York trip. Yet in all things connected with the ship, as far as I could judge, his decisions were swift, direct and usually correct. Life with him could certainly never be dull, and I wondered whether our personalities would clash. I thought not, for against such men I become a nebulous creature, and remain too interested in their personalities and their methods of domination to be subdued; I cannot fight them, having no wish to dominate others. Willoughby said, months later, that 'I was too damned self-contained'. That fact might infuriate him but usually such unobtrusive qualities remain unnoticed by forceful creatures, who are often unobservant concerning personalities which do not clash with their own. I thought we should become a working unit, but I was anxious to watch the effect of the Captain's strong and unconventional personality upon the crew.

Willoughby had been a rolling stone. He had left Harrow at seventeen and had then gone to Aleppo, to the Near Eastern offices of the family business in rare oriental rugs and carpets. With Aleppo as a base, he had travelled throughout Turkey, Syria, Persia and much of Northern Arabia, and he spoke as an expert on the diverse politics of those regions; he had, too, more than a smattering of the *argots* of the Levant. After five years of this wandering life he had fallen in love with the wife of a Swiss watch magnate who was exploring the Levant for new markets. They had met in Damascus; he had followed her back to Berne; she had left her husband and they had lived for two years by Lucerne. His father had then died. During his return to London to clear up the estate, his mistress had returned to her husband, bidding Willoughby to see her no more. He then returned to Syria, working there until the European slump. His business had collapsed, but he had enough money for his needs and his mother had adequate means of her own. He had returned to England to live with her, for she was old and very ill, and, as an extreme contrast to this vegetating life in Sussex, he had taken up motor racing at Brooklands and Donington, but, after his mother's death in 1935, he had returned to the Levant. 'It is probably in my blood,' he said one evening. 'It gets people that way. God knows why! Mosquitoes, dust, too much sun, filthy local habits, a lot of twisting natives, and I hate the French. But there it is. I suppose it is really the only life I knew.' Back in Syria he had lived with a local girl in a villa on the coast between Tripoli and Beirut for two years, and then, on an impulse, he had asked the girl to marry him and return with him to London; but she would not leave the sun for London fogs, and had returned to her father, a wealthy *hotelier* in Beirut. Willoughby had returned to England to become, of all things, a fairly successful stockbroker with a side interest in a small company making profitable documentary films, and, 'oddly enough,' he said, 'those were the two happiest years of my life. I liked the City of London's cloak of respectability for more sin and squalor in a week than the Orient could cough up in a month. I liked my pseudo-intellectual connections with the film world; and I liked my young and beautiful, and struggling film-struck girl friends. They were easy on the eye and easy on the purse – while they were struggling. I want to get back. This war is an interim period.'

That had been, briefly enough, the life of Miles Richard Willoughby. Now, uprooted by the war from his London life, he wished to return to the Mediterranean, but by those strange processes of Admiralty authority he had spent his war in the North Sea and the Atlantic. After service as a junior officer in a Tribal class destroyer at the beginning of the war, he had been transferred to a Hunt class destroyer until the end of 1940. Then he had been made first lieutenant in a corvette, but the appointment had lasted only three months. Now he had been given his own command and was keen to engage upon that career.

'I'm not really keen on this Royal Navy stuff, but it's better than being in a tank or a bomber and one is, at least, one's own boss.'

I agreed, doubting inwardly whether I should be as keen as Willoughby on having my own command, but that was a problem scarcely likely to present itself for several months. Meanwhile there were enough preliminary problems for the first lieutenant to deal with in a ship which had not even put to sea, and I returned once more to the list of daily outstanding tasks which we revised each evening. Always the list lengthened.

❧

Half-way through the third week of our sojourn in Halifax I collected a signal at the base which informed the Commanding Officer, HMS *Tobias*, that Sub-Lieutenant P Richmond, RNVR, and Sub-Lieutenant K G W C Benson, RNVR, were due to join HMS *Tobias* within a few days. They were en route from UK in a fast convoy, said the signals officer. 'It's a relief to know there are such beings abroad somewhere,' said Willoughby, who had begun to doubt the existence of any *very* junior officers for the ship. 'Wonder what Benson's plethora of initials indicate. I suppose he's been known as 'Alphabet' Benson ever since school. He'll be known as that in *Tobias*, anyway.'

They arrived together, four days later.

Sub-Lieutenant Peter Richmond, RNVR, was a round-faced young man, about twenty-six, with thinning hair, a rotund figure, and smiling, intelligent eyes. He was shy and self-possessed, combining those contradictory qualities in a manner peculiar to many undergraduates. Sub-Lieutenant Keith Gracechurch Welsh Charles Benson, RNVR, might have been any age between twenty-five and forty and was also round-faced, but his was the dark, bland, smiling face of an oriental. 'Just like one of those charming crooks I had to deal with years ago in the bazaars of Istanbul,' said Willoughby in a hissed aside as we walked along the deck. 'Smooth customer, I should think.'

At the sight of the two officers staggering across the quay from the works office, obviously bound for *Tobias*, we had stopped a desultory discussion with an electrician on the upper bridge. The electrician had been explaining details concerning certain improvements to the asdic apparatus which he had perfected and which 'the Admiralty here won't look at'. His explanation, delivered whilst he was supervising the final stages of fixing our conventional system, had contained much venom and was delivered with the glowering resentment of the ignored inventor. It had been an involved, technical and far from convincing exposition to my untechnical mind, and I was glad to escape, to hail the two voyagers and welcome them aboard.

They staggered across one of the narrow planks which served as gangways to the ship. I smiled to note the alacrity with which they dumped their gear and saluted their new ship as they stepped on board. They had obviously remembered *King Alfred* drill most adequately.

'Have a good trip?' said Willoughby.

'Yessir,' they said together.

A general series of introductions followed. Then Willoughby suggested we should go below. He showed them into their cabin. They were appreciative. 'Like a noggin?' the Captain asked. 'You'll probably need one after coping with the base wallahs.' They agreed. It was a sharp morning, but both were sweating like draymen. They peeled off their greatcoats and hurled them on to the bare bunks. We all went into the wardroom, which was quickly becoming an almost stylish withdrawing-room under the efforts of Jake, the steward.

'This is very pleasant,' said Richmond.

'We have a man of taste as steward,' said the Captain, 'and, more important, I think the bogey stove will work in winter.' He poured impressive measures of whiskey into tumblers, adding minute dashes of water, and began to ask them about their trip, to compare it with our own; then the conversation moved to the previous seafaring experience of the two juniors.

Richmond had been three months in a trawler as a sort of combined Number Two and supernumerary. He confessed to little experience apart from that: he had a technical interest in gunnery and navigation which derived, he thought, from a certain facility in mathematical studies. Benson had been, for about five months, in a vintage destroyer on east coast escort work. He had been A/S officer – the officer in charge of anti-submarine warfare – but as there had been few submarines in the North Sea and his destroyer had not encountered one of the few, he had been badgering his commanding officer and the base for a chance of transferring to the Atlantic, which he considered the proving-ground for what skill he had. Apart from that he had little experience. He had done no watchkeeping in the destroyer, he said dismally, and knew little enough, but he was keen to learn. 'My ship was Captain D's tub,' he said viciously, 'and the ship was lousy with officers and specialists. Too much humph, gold braid, stiff collars and gin. We spent most of our time having refits and swinging round the buoy. Every time we came into harbour rude fellows in other ships in the flotilla used to lean over the sides of their ships and yell "'ere comes the bleedin' 'otel!" Gets a chap down. Got me down, anyway. Spent most of my time writing plays for the ship's company to perform. The day I saw my name listed in the Captain's orders of the day as "Entertainments Officer" I knew it was time for me to gird up my loins and depart. Besides, I wanted to get a watchkeeping certificate. Not much use in being in the Navy without that, is there? Might as well be a coastguard. So once every week I put in for a transfer to a corvette. I got a bit unpopular with the CO but here I am.' We chatted on until lunch-time. I watched the Captain drawing out the two officers, learning something of them as men, estimating their worth as potential officers in *Tobias*. Benson was animated, sophisticated and self-assured. In conversation he moved his hands in easy gestures. His dark eyes sparkled.

He spoke for effect. He had achieved those effects before, and knew he would achieve them again. He had no great wish to impress, I judged, but rather to entertain. Richmond listened. He was quiet, content to let his companion entertain. He laughed at the recital and said his own adventures had been dull in comparison. 'I was in a small patrol craft in the Solent and we did a small job. There was a chance to learn and then I was transferred. It was as simple as that.'

We all went across to the canteen for lunch. Over the meal they were both keen to know more about corvettes, the manner of life, dress, work in these unromantic craft. Willoughby and myself took turns in answering this quick-fire questionnaire. After lunch Willoughby gave them a chance to see the town. 'Pity not to see something of every new port.'

Willoughby and myself spent most of the afternoon walking and rewalking the seventy or eighty yards of quay apportioned to HMS *Tobias* since we had come from the slipways for fitting-out. Willoughby was keen to get a rough division of labour amongst the ship's four watchkeeping officers before the main body of the crew arrived on the following day. They had probably travelled out with Richmond and Benson, he surmised, and were already billeted in the base. Several of the specialist ratings might descend upon us at any moment and we ought to be prepared for their arrival. He talked at length. I knew he was clarifying his mind by using my own as a sort of coffee grinder into which he threw his odd beans of projects. Inexpert in the task, I ground them mildly but helped to give him the results he wanted. Our conversation turned over many possibilities in the future life of HMS *Tobias*. Slight excerpts come back to me as I recall the grey port, cluttered quay and many workmen moving and working upon the ship.

WILLOUGHBY: What do you know about gunnery, Number One? You say you know very little. Is that true or the usual British modesty stuff?

MYSELF: I know very little. I did my gunnery course at *KA,* and could probably train and knock a gun's crew into shape, but I'm not an expert.

WILLOUGHBY: You *could* take over the four-inch, then?

MYSELF: Yes, of course.

WILLOUGHBY: You'd have Petty Officer Campbell to help.

MYSELF: If he needs any help. What help does a pukka 'Guns' need from me?

WILLOUGHBY: It's a division of responsibilities, really, Number One. Would you rather have the depth charge crews?

MYSELF: I think I know more about depth charges.

WILLOUGHBY: That's true. Wonder what Richmond's like on his gunnery.

MYSELF: He looks as if he'd be reliable in anything he took up.

WILLOUGHBY: Damn the English. You can never judge them from their own statements of their qualifications. Richmond may be a ballistics expert for all he'd say on the subject. Thank God it's obvious that Benson must know something about A/S work. Solves one of the major problems, anyway. Actually we're rather lucky to get a full-blown U-boat king. He must be that. I think you'd better be pilot, Number One, with Richmond as your winger. I think you'd better have the depth charges, too. We can change later if necessary.

MYSELF: What about watches?

WILLOUGHBY: You and I had better work watch-andwatch for the first couple of months. It'll be rather wearing, but we'll just have to take it. We can see how we go for standing watches after that. It's going to be tolerably tough now and then.

Throughout the afternoon we talked, trying to work out our own minute plan for war-making within that great framework made by statesmen, politicians and strategists.

We were getting to know each other, too, and that was as important as growth in knowledge of our ship.

That evening Willoughby dined with his friend, the Canadian colonel, and I dined at the Green Lantern with Richmond and Benson. In the usual manner of all amateur sailors we were soon talking about the war: at greater length about our jobs before the war and at greatest length about what we would do after the war.

Richmond was obviously an idealist of the most engaging kind: gentle, slightly self-deprecating, intelligent. His major interest was politics. He had been president of the Union and was preoccupied by thoughts of the masses. He spoke of The Workers gently and remotely, as if he were some grand designer, master of their fate, a characteristic often seen in youthful reformers. He might prove an infuriating goad to a dialectical opponent, I thought, and visualised some hectic wardroom debates if the Captain and Richmond began to compare their respective estimates of human nature. I hoped to be there, and wondered how much of Richmond's outlook was sincere and how much was the result of Oxford theorising. He had been an architect in civil life and had started his own practice, breaking away from his father's well-established firm about a year before the war. In this way we began to talk about architecture. Like many other intellectually inclined creatures caught into war he was grateful for the chance of discussion. He had spoken of architecture only once during his time in trawlers, he said. His ship had been the peacetime command of her wartime skipper, 'a most worthy old soul, but for him architects were people who put up statues and art galleries. When I told him I designed houses he said he thought builders did that, and what could an architect do that a builder couldn't?'

Benson had been trained as a professional seaman. He had been sent to the *Worcester* at fourteen, but owing to a defect in his eyesight, not apparent in his earliest medical examinations, he had been presented, at the age of sixteen, with the alternatives of becoming an engineer officer in the Merchant Service or of quitting. He had left and gone to an uncle's farm in Kenya, but he hated open air life. 'God, how I hate those vast sweeps of unspoiled landscape,' he said. He had returned to London and become, by devious methods, a successful furrier; then he had gone into the catering business. Again he had been successful. With the income he derived from these activities he had backed a ballet company, 'or, more accurately, one of the dancers in the company, a rather muscular brunette, as I remember,' he said and smiled. This patronage had cost him much money, I gathered, but he was the complete sophisticate, and must have remained unperturbed. Now, during the war, his fur and food interests were being controlled by his partner, a Swiss Jew. 'Completely honest, oddly enough,' said Benson in conclusion, and from this I inferred that he was likely to be by far the most affluent member of our wardroom.

I was puzzled by Benson. There were contrasts and contradictions in his character and confessions. He admitted that he had not volunteered for the Navy at the outbreak of war, but had been called up and had then been granted a commission on the basis of his early training. Yet he had volunteered for the Atlantic when he might have kept to his 'soft number' on the east coast, with its frequent trips to London. He was as assured, bright-eyed, black-haired, suave and brassy as a music-hall manager. He was obviously a born salesman, and I was almost persuaded that he was Jewish, or partly Jewish. His chatter and tales were amusing, and his gift for mimicry enlivening, but I found myself resenting my susceptibility to these qualities in him. I put such resentment down to his oriental appearance, but, with Richmond, I laughed immoderately at his anecdotes of London balletomanes and furriers, intrigued by the bright foreign colours he introduced into the small world of a warship. There was, too, the prospect that the Captain's reactions to Benson's personality might be more graphic than his reactions to Richmond's beliefs in the worker's world of tomorrow. My interest in people and their characters would have scope, I thought, for a small warship is an adequate setting for assembling a widely differing caste. After a voluble supper we went off to see Mr William Powell and Miss Carole Lombard in a wildly hilarious film about butlers and the upper strata of New Yorkers. Miss Lombard seemed alluring but both she and New York seemed poignantly remote from Halifax, said Benson, who had also spent two days in the Barbizon-Plaza.

❧

The crew also arrived from Britain and now as Number One I had to begin to get to grips with the men. From the moment that they came on board as a draft the work began. First, there was the sizing-up stage. I had them 'fallen in' on the quayside by the coxswain on the afternoon of their arrival, and after the Captain had spoken to them briefly but pleasantly and had then retired, I walked their lines to find out what sort of men *Tobias* would have to man her. Whether this was normal naval procedure I could not tell. Almost all that we did was done in such circumstances, improvising, for we had no precedents to remember, no long years of naval curriculum to consult within our minds. So I questioned them, asking normal naval questions and often receiving far-from-normal naval replies.

'Name?'

'Higgs, sir.'

'What base?'

'Chatham, sir.'

'Been to sea before?'

'No, sir.'

'Why did you join the Navy?'

'Me old man was in it in the last war, sir.'

'What did you do in civvy street?'

'Barrer boy in Bermondsey, sir.'

(Momentarily puzzled I recovered quickly: 'barrow boy'.)

'Have a good trip? Any complaints?'

'Not bad, sir. They charged us for food coming up in the train from New York, sir. When we was coming through the States. Dollar each for each meal, sir. Bit thick, we thought.'

'You'll get that back. Petty Officer Reynolds will make a note of the amounts and draw from the Base "pay" here.' ('Pay' is the naval abbreviation for the paymaster officer, from whom officers and men drew the casual payments which kept us going and on which keep all Royal Navy crews subsist when ashore abroad. The amounts drawn are entered upon local ledgers and in paybooks and thence forwarded to the accountant officer at the Home Base against a later, sinister day of reckoning.)

The trades and professions on that quayside in Halifax made a strange assembly: barrow boy, two printers, stationer's assistant, two railway workers ('Why did you leave the railway? Isn't it a reserved occupation?' and in both instances, 'Wanted to get into the Navy, sir. Wasn't keen on being reserved'), bricklayer, glass blower, bus conductor, several clerks, two sons of farmers, a cobbler, a barber (lucky is the ship that has a professional barber on board!), milkman, waiter, garage mechanic, and a dozen other callings. Inevitably there were one or two superior answers to my question concerning pre-war career:

'Meat salesman, sir,' said one tall, dark, swarthy newcomer with knife-edge creases in his bell bottoms.

'Did you sell meat or could you handle meat in the galley?'

'I sold meat, sir.'

'In a market or shop?'

'In a multiple shop, sir.'

'Could you handle meat in the galley?'

'I could, sir, but I am primarily a salesman.'

I was too abashed by such distinctions in the trade to ask whether he ever had to touch or even to wrap the meat he sold. From another I got the reply: 'Insurance salesman, sir.'

'In an office or outside?'

'Colchester, sir. I had built up my own connection in East Anglia.'

'What's happened to it now?'

'My wife is carrying on, sir.'

'Any children?'

'Two, sir.'

I said briefly, 'Good for her', and wondered how many other dogged stories their simple answers covered. Their mail which would soon be piling on the wardroom table would tell us so that we should know which of the men took grim thoughts with them upon watch, which of them memories of philandering, which of them hopes, which of them fears.

The full complement of HMS *Tobias* was almost seventy: five officers, three chief petty officers, and sixty petty officers and men. Of these almost one-third were engine-room staff; asdic and communications accounted for nine, cooks and stewards still further diminished the essential core of the crew. From the earliest days we were deep in that dilemma which is focused before every Captain before he begins his seagoing life in command: how to seize every possible man for deck duties, and always the dilemma has unsatisfactory answer: that there is never a sufficient number of men for deck, for watches, for fighting, for the hundred and one tasks that must keep a ship fully manned as a thoroughgoing man-o'-war.

We quickly discovered that Benson was a technical expert in asdic as well as a trained operator, and the misanthropic inventor had a shock the day following his diatribe to Willoughby and myself, for Benson began to discuss his scheme with ruthless scientific detachment, or so it appeared to me, a lay eavesdropper. The inventor listened, nodded sagely and left the ship that afternoon very quietly, visibly shaken. Benson was maliciously delighted, and continued his analysis with me as audience, talking of 'correct polarity', 'oscillators', 'junction boxes', 'valves', and other mechanical usages with fluency until he realised that I knew little more about the asdic than the ship's cook. I could operate the device but the precise reasons how or why it worked were far beyond me. Benson was kinder with my ignorance than with the inventor's genius. I began to realise that our tame furrier was amongst those handymen who believe in knowing everything about the interiors of their motor cars, wireless sets, refrigerators and torches. I am not of that select and invaluable coterie.

Six asdic ratings arrived during the afternoon. They had been in the draft but had been misdirected, an inevitable occurrence at such times. They reported to me, for the Captain was ashore, and I passed them over to Benson, who took them over with avuncular yet rigid discipline. They would be his disciples but also his slaves, his manner implied. He was jocular yet firm, combining his talent for the grand manner with a complete lack of its normally attendant pomposity. I returned to the chart folios which I had been examining with Richmond. Leaning over the small chart table I could hear the steady lecture being delivered in a genially hectoring tone by Benson. I turned from the table to go below. Benson's men were deeply occupied by the apparatus, which was housed in a steel-plated cabinet on the starboard side of the bridge-house. He had just given them a poser. They were profoundly puzzled. Over their hunched shoulders he gave me a slow and solemn wink. Benson obviously had no intention of taking his grand manner very grandly. The realisation came to me that basically he was a clever and insinuating actor and with that discovery much of his manner was explained. He would be amusing to watch. I grinned, as I crossed the quay to speak to one of the foremen.

❧

Now, as I approached the ship from the yard, across the quay, or left the ship to go ashore and looked back, I could see that *Tobias* was almost a ship, almost shaped to a recognisable profile, no longer a mass of plates and unrelated engines, no longer a dead and empty hull with dull metal parts lying placeless on the quay. *Tobias* was almost built.

❧

Two days later our initial tasks were almost done. On that day the ship was officially handed over to the Royal Navy by the contractors. A 'brass-hat' from the base was present, obviously very competent and experienced in the handling of such ceremonies. Various officials from the shipbuilding company also attended. A superhet 5-valve wireless receiver was given by the shipbuilders to the crew of HMS *Tobias,* a smaller set and a glittering canteen of cutlery to the wardroom. Modest and generous speeches were made. All present at the party contained in their eyes the light of good fellowship and peace. Willoughby forgot his violent condemnation of the contractors made to the managing director and works manager a fortnight before. The managing director spoke of HMS *Tobias* and her gallant officers and men as if we were direct lineal descendants of Frobisher, Drake and Nelson.

The local brass-hat spoke of the records of corvettes already built by the yard. 'In fact, only the bride and bridegroom were missing,' said the Captain afterwards, but we were all too busy watching Dundass fixing our superhet, and listening to Benson's airily and freely given expert advice, to wish to add to the Captain's cynicism. 'This,' said Dundass, 'is a wireless set an' a half. We'll be getting Moscoo the noo.'

❧

Final fittings and trials remained, but these were important and it seemed that we might have to make our homeward journey without the multiple pom-poms aft, 'although we probably shan't need them much. We're scarcely likely to run into Focke Wulfs in the North Atlantic,' Willoughby said.

The following morning we watched, from the bridge, the shipping and fixing of our four-inch gun. Five minutes before we had been a hull, christened, it is true, but a bluff, pacific hull. Now, within the hours of morning, we had become a warship. Previously I had joined ships which were, in the requirements of Their Lordships, 'in all respects ready for war'. Now, watching the addition of a major 'respect' to our own accoutrements, I was heartened.

'Guns' was Petty Officer Jonathan Campbell, twenty-six, a long-service man who had been living for this moment. He watched the crane during the lowering of the gun-mounting with tense and anxious eyes.

'She looks a nice job, sir,' he said half an hour later. 'A nineteen-eighteen Vickers job. Brand new breech rings. Think there's one or two items – the gudgeons and recoil cylinder – I'd like to have a look-see with the armourer, if that's in order, sir.'

'He's coming aboard tomorrow morning, Campbell. He says at ten o'clock. You'd better be ready to take him over.'

'Aye, aye, sir. There's the trunnion locking blocks, too. I'd like a word about them, too, sir.'

'With me, Campbell?' I asked, dread perhaps implicit in my voice, for he smiled, saying, 'No, sir. The armourer.'

'You have full permission, Campbell, to discuss gudgeons and trunnions with the base armourer from ten in the morning until midnight on condition you keep me out of the discussion.'

'Aye, aye, sir.'

'And you'll be glad to hear we're getting our pom-poms,' I said, handing him a signal.

His joy was as if I had offered him a four-inch gun cast in gold especially for himself.

Campbell's salute as he left my cabin was exact, buoyant, boding no peace for an unsuspecting armourer. Such things, I knew, I could leave in the capable hands of the specialists, but there were other aspects of life in *Tobias* which, I knew, could not be so successfully sidestepped. The safety of the ship at sea, for instance, became one of my greater cares. Flooding is an ominous possibility in any ship, particularly in escort work, with prospects and dangers of collision in blacked-out roadsteads. Watertight discipline, the use of pumps and a complete knowledge of the ship's ventilation system become a matter of almost academic concern to the First Lieutenant. Prospect of fire is another nightmare and I read up all notes I could find on fire by oil fuel, fire by diesel oil, fire by petrol, fire by paintwork, woodwork, bedding. I read with outward calm but inward qualms the simple understatements of instruction: 'When shells, bombs and torpedoes explode there is a large, intensely hot, momentary flash', or 'Fire is always accompanied by dense smoke, so be prepared for it by knowing your ship so well that you can find your way in darkness, and by knowing how to use the breathing apparatus provided, so that you can remain in the smoke and fight the fires'.

Similar instructions were recorded, I remembered, in the *Instructions Issued to Seamen by Authority of The Lords Commissioners of The Admiralty,* and I could only hope that those gallant souls were also assiduous in their book learning.

There were less dramatic but even more terrifying details on my list. I would be responsible for much of the crew's discipline and neatness. A simple, straightforward inspection of the men's kit, for instance, would present me with many moments of trepidation: in the muster would I be certain whether black boots were placed adjacent to greatcoat or to jumper? Already, in prospect, I felt the sceptical eyes of the Petty Officer of the Day upon me as I made rounds, nervously aware of my nautical solecisms and presumptions.

I began once more to dip into *King's Regulations and Admiralty Instructions,* that volume of naval lore and knowledge. I had dipped into its pages before, for entertainment: now I began to read with prodigious devotion. I was anxious to acquire, within a few weeks, the know ledge which seeps into the very veins of RN officers in their long journey from Dartmouth to the bridge. Many of the items to which I gave attention were scarcely likely, it seemed, to be of momentous importance in my future life as a 'Jimmy', but from others, promulgated in that dignified typographical style favoured by His Majesty's Stationery Office, I learned that the truly efficient officer must be certain 'to see that all on board subordinate to him perform their duties with diligence and propriety. He is to check all profane swearing, and improper or obscene language; and all disturbances, noise or confusion'; and that 'at sea he is to be extremely careful to keep station with other ships, and is to report at once if unable to do so'.

Most of these instructions applied to all officers on board. One or two were delightful examples of understatement. Under the heading of Important Occurrences, I noted that the officer of the watch 'is to inform the Captain, or cause him to be informed, of all strange vessels seen'. This would be only too promptly obeyed, I thought, if I should suddenly see the strange shape of a conning-tower rising from the deep.

I also read through the many paragraphs of instructions to Captains, reading them fearfully and fleetingly, unwishful that a close reading of them would soon be necessary, but that dread, I knew, need not be with me for months, and I turned with relief to other sections, particularly to that chapter headed 'Pay and Allowances, cash, victualling, stores and pensions'. The complicated paragraphs of this section are guaranteed to keep any naval officer quietly engrossed for an evening. Other evenings would be as full, I knew, for under the heading of 'Officers (Generally)' the Index to the *King's Regulations* records almost seventy Articles and Clauses of Articles, ranging from 'Assemblages of Officers – rule as to precedence at – (see Precedence)' to 'Divine Service – officers – attendance at'; from 'Marriage – officers – notification of – (see Marriages)' to 'Officers – unfit or unworthy of further employment; powers in regard to 510 App XIII.'

The book learning demanded of a First Lieutenant seemed almost the most onerous of his tasks, I often told myself, switching off the cabin light, and turning to slumbers complicated by dreams of surrealistic situations provoked and developed in *Tobias* by a misunderstanding of the uneasy sentences of officialese.

Chapter 4

The Continuing Battle

A watery sun ('as pallid and shrivelled as a northern nun,' said Benson) gave us scant heart during our last day in Halifax. The crew moved about the quayside and the ship, taking stores on board and stowing gear, like shameless stevedores in a forsaken port. There was no likeness of warriors in them. Their working rig, too, diminished their heroic stature for they wore mainly dungarees or sweaters, and a miscellany of headgear which would have attracted (perhaps even predatorily) Mr Churchill. An ordinary seaman, moving from the quayside to the ship, wore a pillar-box-red balaclava with bright blue pom-pom. I called to him, having found in *Solander* that a way to memorise the names of the ship's company was to use their names upon the slightest cause, and if in doubt to call, even peremptorily, 'That man, there!' or some equally noxious cry, and then, in querying an errand or a task, ask his name, thus striving to hold the name against the future. I found no zest in this *memoria technica*, but wished to have names to my lips as soon as possible, certainly before we quit the port, and, to gain this end, the method seemed permissible.

The necessity for memorising the names and faces of the crew is important for the First Lieutenant in any warship. Much of his life must be spent in giving the men orders, listening to their woeful accounts of the misdeeds of Their Lordships and other notabilities of the Admiralty (particularly the Director of Naval Accounts), and, quite often, in asking those same seamen for advice, for he must be a pontifical First Lieutenant indeed, who never yet sought knowledge from at least one or two experienced members of his crew. Because such orders are given and such requests are made more easily by name, naval officers are adjured in *King's Regulations and Admiralty Instructions* to learn the names of their crew as quickly as possible. Whilst in *Solander* I had read the appropriate paragraph, phrased in sturdy officialese, and smiled to think that now, in my fashion, I was obeying these instructions.

My call had brought the gaily headgeared OS before me. I asked his name.

'Myers, sir.'

'Which watch?'

'Blue watch, sir.'

'What are you about now?'

'Quartermaster wants some more sugar, sir. Says he thinks we're a bit short.'

'How much extra there?'

'One hundredweight, sir.'

'Very good, Myers. Carry on.'

'Aye, aye, sir.'

Such attention to domestic details boded well for our food, for these factors formed much of the background to our daily lives, and a reader of these pages should know that the question of sugar was as important in our lives as the question of ammunition for the four-inch gun. I had confidence in any quartermaster who showed sagacity in these early days, remembering that a boat's crew in *Solander* had once dropped a hundredweight of sugar overboard after a rash attempt to swing the sack on deck from a bobbing whaler. The Captain had blistered them; there had been no time to return to the base ship for more, and we had sailed with no extra store. Before the end of the trip we were regretful, for our 'spotted dog' puddings came from the galley as effective but unsweetened stop-gaps, not those gastronomic joys which had made us sybarites on previous trips.

I climbed to the bridge and watched and listened to the turmoil of the yard. The last day alongside is always a medley and a babel. Donkey engines jabbered and racketed in their mechanical dance; acetylene burners hissed around the gun platform; hammers crashed dully upon wood, clanged against metal. Voices rose in catcalls and in orders against the tumult. The air was vibrant with the epileptic din.

Scanning the men, I realised that for many of them the true battle of the Atlantic was now to begin. Although they might not think of it in such high-flown terms, the thought that they might soon know more of that sombre scene came often to their minds, to judge from words sometimes overheard. They had been in training establishments ashore, they had crossed the Atlantic in a troopship, but now they knew, if they thought upon the matter at all, that their real life as seamen was upon them. Richmond, censor officer, had said the previous evening in the wardroom that, to judge from their final letters home, many of them seemed aware of the immensity of the task ahead, and of the possibility of trials and perhaps sorrow. They brooded upon these things, but seemed not profoundly perturbed, he said. They seemed to think only of the effect of loss upon their families and upon family finances, scarcely ever of themselves; and because Richmond was sensitive to these things it was obvious that he pondered upon the social backgrounds of the crew. I could imagine him reflecting upon the taut conflicts and cramped ways of life implicit in the inarticulate scribbles. 'There is a good deal of tragedy underlying any mail,' he said, after a pause. 'Inevitable, I suppose. One of the men in this ship left a child in England aged three and destined to die of consumption in three months. His wife is almost half crazy, judging by the way he writes to keep her hopeful. Yet he doesn't know, never learned how to do these things in a letter. All he can say is "Perhaps she won't die. Perhaps the doctor was wrong." I suppose, with public school backgrounds, we could do the job better. It's their terrifying inability to express themselves.' He went on. There was little we could do. We had all censored mail in our time at sea.

Midway through the morning Willoughby was requested by signal to report to the base for final instructions. He rejoined us at lunch, saying briefly that we would get out into the stream during the early afternoon, for a coaster was due to take our berth alongside at 1500 hours, and we must leave long before that time if we valued the name of our ship and our own reputation as mariners about the port. We went from the wardroom and strolled aft. I asked the time of our departure. He said the following morning.

'Does morning mean dawn?'

'No, not till nine-thirty, thank God. We can get our heads down tonight.'

I asked whether there were many ships in the convoy.

'Fairly large. About three dozen merchantmen, I think. I shall know better this afternoon after the Masters' conference.'

'Many escorts?'

'Too few,' he said. 'I suppose they just haven't got 'em. They do their best, but we could do with another half-dozen escorts for this convoy alone. Two destroyers, two corvettes, two trawlers and ourselves. I suppose we should count as a corvette in the book, but I don't think we can give ourselves that dignity just yet.'

It was scarcely reassuring to meditate upon the prospect before us. As a race we are too easy in our memories, and I find in myself this distaste for recollection of the drearier occasions of those earlier days. We put memories of perilous times aside as if they were peculiar, inconsequential intrusions into our normal tale, unlikely to recur and therefore not worth recalling. Yet now, in writing these words and in the slow endeavour of my story, I remember our awareness of the awaiting enemy, and our simple knowledge that we should not escape him. Across a distance placed by many months I sense again our querying preoccupation with our leaden speeds, my sometimes doleful wonderings, my uncompounded hatred of the sea.

❧

At that time, the late Spring of 1941, the Atlantic Battle was in a crucial phase. Those many U-boats which had been laid down in the German shipyards in 1939 and 1940 were coming into service. This we learned from paragraphs in documents headed 'secret' which occasionally we were enabled to read. The enemy, said the reports with admirable and almost academic detachment, could maintain thirty-five U-boats at sea, most of them in the North and West Atlantic. To judge from plotted charts seen sometimes in the base, the U-boats seemed to be operating at will in almost every area of the ocean used by our shipping. They were getting bolder, too, operating close to the Newfoundland coast where the convoys gathered or dispersed.

In May, Admiral Doenitz, the German Admiral Commanding U-boats, had shifted his forces to the South Atlantic. His men had worked off Freetown with success and in the approaches to the Cape Verde Islands, but many attacks had also been made upon Allied shipping within a few hundred miles of the Canadian coast. The Admiralty had decided to use what was termed the 'end-to-end' convoy system, which meant that escorts convoyed their charges from port to port. Before, in *Solander,* we had worked to 25 degrees West with one convoy, and then, at a rendezvous, had taken charge of another convoy for escorting back to England. Now, it seemed, losses were so monotonously impressive, the need so urgent, that other means must counter German tactics, despite the desperate lack of escorts. The enemy was so numerous that he might be found at any point between Newfoundland and Skerryvore, between Iceland and Freetown. Warships, therefore, must cross the ocean from end to end.

We heard a rumour that the preceding eastward convoy had been badly mauled by a pack of U-boats, that five or six ships had been sunk, the battle lasting through four nights. We could not learn the truth. Gossip in the port was too wild, authentic sources too few, for us to sift the truth from hearsay. Willoughby said that if only there were one local clearing-house for truth, however grim, our lives might be made less complex and, in many ways, less apprehensive. Always, he contended, there should be one room for truth. 'It is little enough to ask Their Lordships. God knows, but they don't seem keen for us to know what is sunk, what isn't, and where and when. Do they think we should spread it abroad?' but I could put no answers to his questions.

Against recurring pessimism was also reassuring gossip, for sailors must often delude themselves with rosier views. Many of the aces who had begun the U-boat campaign under Doenitz in 1939 had been killed or captured. Many of the 1941 U-boat crews were 'green', diluted with Nazi youth, fervent in new orders of philosophy but unskilled in older orders of seamanship and navigation. The sceptics among us, however, accepted these theories with reserve, placing technical improvements in U-boats as machines for sinking and killing against possibilities of inexpert handling, and finding the odds against us. Willoughby and myself had seen something of the U-boat's power to cut a convoy to ribbons, and we sometimes smiled in disbelief when we heard the glib words.

~❧

We shifted *Tobias* into the stream during that afternoon, and worked through to the evening to get her fully shipshape. Many problems arise in the last moments before weighing anchor and Willoughby, myself and Chief Petty Officer Reynolds moved from bow to stern, overseeing, adjusting, revising, deciding. We left Reynolds by the after hold where much stowing was still to be done.

'He's good, thank God,' said Willoughby. 'Always one wonders whether the Chiefs will be as good as they can be, and always they are.' I agreed, for Reynolds seemed in the tradition. He was a man of middle height, almost forty. His face was as dark as a Spaniard's; his eyes were clear, grey, cold. The years had cut deeply into his lean cheeks. His voice was harsh and sharp; his orders were swiftly, competently given, and, for his officers, reassuring to hear. His humour was sardonic and merciless.

Yet already I had seen that this man, upon whom so much responsibility would fall, was reasonable and just with men and in dividing tasks about the ship. Already I had heard that simple cry, always expectant of an answer or solution: 'Chief! Where d'you want this 'ere 'awser, chief', or, 'Think we'll get ashore tonight, chief?' Always 'Chief!'

We turned in early. Benson and Richmond were to share the anchor watches and we settled to our last Canadian supper. I remembered similar suppers eaten in *Solander* on the nights before we joined our convoys; gargantuan feasts, almost with a party air about them. So, in *Tobias,* we began our 'First Last Supper' (as Benson irreverently termed it) with that same note of splendour. Jake, the cook, did his best and we sat down to tomato soup, roast chicken, roast potatoes, peas, salad, pears, ice-cream, cheese and coffee.

'When in Canada eat as the Canucks do. That's my motto, sir,' said Jake to the Captain as he brought stupendous pears surrounded by ice-cream tipped with wafers and brightest green angelica.

'And when at sea eat as the fishes do, I suppose?' said Willoughby; but Jake was non-committal and smiling, returned to the galley. 'Drink up!' said Willoughby, 'your last chance. The chest will be closed at midnight and Number One gets the key, and you all know what a mean-gutted so-and-so he is when it comes to liquor.'

They had started with whiskeys, veered towards gins and now finished with brandies. All seemed able to deal with such miscellanies, only the wonderful red of Dundass' cheeks grew perhaps a shade more colorific: only his jaw out-jutted a shade more pugnaciously, yet he was as sober as a bishop, as gently quiet as a resident in an almshouse. At the supper's end, Willoughby, almost with ceremony, handed me the keys.

'Leave one tot of brandy for Alphabet, and then farewell to Bacchante. Goodnight all!'

'Goodnight, sir!' said his junior officers. I went out and up to the bridge to see how Benson was enjoying his first watchkeeping in *Tobias*. The night was dark, an ill-favoured wind came coldly from the inland plains, and even the lights of Halifax seemed dimmed as if to prepare us for the gloom of, first, the sea, and then the British blackout.

Benson was loudly humming a theme from *The Nutcracker Suite*. I told him a brandy awaited him below. 'On the Old Man's chit,' I added.

'Good! Make it a double. It's as cold as my mother's parlourmaid up here.'

⚓

The convoy would be large and slow. That was evident from the lines of the merchantmen. How ably and quickly one learned the essential factors of marine architecture after appraising a dozen convoys! The heavy smoke curdling from the funnels of a sturdy six-thousand tonner ('Not very helpful if that chap can't get that down,' from Willoughby); the wallowing motion of a beamy middleweight too old by ten years for this sort of battle; the high-riding of a tanker too lightly loaded down in Tampico. Even with no previous knowledge of mercantile ways and estimates I came to know some signs of inadequacy and compromise.

We rounded them up. The routine was no different from assemblies off the Northern Irish coast. There were the same stragglers, the same dullards, the same swift willingness. All convoys were the same yet each was different. Finally the pattern was complete and the fleet of antique warriors moved off upon the long voyage home. Willoughby watched from the bridge; 'Bunts' and the second 'Sparks' attending him. The

Captain was quiet, efficient, unhurried; orders were precise, and almost leisurely, but the edge to his voice gave authority to drawled instructions. Now and then he slipped from this conversational approach, but even his words, 'Damn that tanker skipper, what's he think he's playing at?' were an ejaculation of inquiry rather than imprecation.

The sea carried a slow, heavy swell. Cumulus rose above the continent we left, moving in simple yet stupendous stateliness above our fleet. The day was already cold with the chill of the ocean added to the wind. I termed myself a fool to have left my sweater below. 'Keep her at one hundred and twenty, chief,' I said, for it was my watch, and for hours ahead *Tobias* would be almost my very own.

❧

Night closed us in. Clouds, low about us, heavy with rain, raced eastwards before a chiding wind. We envied them their speed and freedom. They would not wait for slow encumbrances. Sometimes one oversped another in their tumbling flight, and momentary gaps opened to show us the thin moon and the cold small light of Jupiter, but the gaps closed quickly, and once more I had that slightest touch of claustrophobia within the immeasurable ocean. The clouds, the night, the near horizon, closed us into such a small arena. It was strange, I often thought, that such sensations could ever come in the Atlantic, but I think that other sailors have been impressed by this seeming paradox of oppression by space. Perhaps peacetime sailors never knew this sensation, except in storm. Perhaps the unceasing fear of U-boats helped to strengthen the impression.

The seas were heavy, raising us high, letting us down in uneasy motion so that our screws kicked against the insubstantial air, whirring, shocking the body, unused in recent weeks to such harsh usage, such sickening pauses upon the sea's high edge.

At night, the ship itself became detached, forced more completely into its own existence, almost sundered from the convoy in which it steamed, and, when storm or fog came with the night, this sense of isolation was yet more insistent. Those flashed aldis signals which enlivened our days, usually in query from or to the commodore or senior escort, but sometimes in ribald derision or complaint between two ships, would pink the night only in crisis. We moved upon our concerted zig-zag patterns like well-drilled units upon a barrack square, but only the pattern was imposed. The life of the ship moved individually into its own way. Only peril would bring us once more together. It was certain that, for this reason, older masters in many merchantmen welcomed the night. If crisis came and they were forced to disperse they would be unperturbed, rejoice indeed, for many were still convinced that they would make a better job of crossing the Atlantic by independent sailing, than in convoy.

I made the black-out rounds with the Petty Officer of the watch on deck, examining the hatches, the engine-room flaps, the wardroom and mess-deck scuttles with minute care. On the first night out a sudden wafer of light from one of the merchantmen loomed across the path of the convoy like a flash from a lightship. Such a light could be seen for miles, and Willoughby's curse upon the bridge was fierce as we swung towards the outer line of the convoy so that he might more effectively damn the master of the officer of the watch for such madness.

This, then, was our night: men above, staring, directing, listening; men below, sleeping, tending, listening.

We passed through the dangerous areas off the Canadian and Newfoundland coasts. During three days Sunderlands flew in vast circles around the convoy, watched over us and then were seen no more. By the seventh day we were moving slowly towards the middle of the ocean. The heavy seas slowed down an already too-slow convoy, and there were stragglers amongst the ships. These we searched for and rounded up in the dawn, cursing their patchwork boilers and their optimistic masters, but our curses were to soothe our feelings and held no venom, for we knew something of the task with which many of the engineer officers of the merchantmen must grapple unceasingly. They had steamed in days of peace with wheezing engines and spraying pipes, grumbled at the parsimony of owners and carried on. Now, in those same ships, they added to their enlivening diurnal tasks knowledge of their likely fate if their engines failed and their ships should fall astern.

I watched the crew about their jobs, particularly the six communications ratings: three 'Bunts' and three 'Sparks', for if the life of the nation might depend in great part upon the Royal Navy, it was certain that our own minute part of the Navy might depend upon sound communications. The men seemed equal to their tasks, technically, and, perhaps more important, as men.

Amongst the 'Sparks' was Ross, a London Scot, a tall, dark, awkward creature with a lopsided face and a gash of a smile. He had pretensions to the Higher Education, for he had attended many sessions of London County Council evening classes, and he combined his erudition with political opinions inclined far to the Left. Donovan, a young Irishman, whose parents had moved ten years before from his birthplace, Dublin, to Liverpool, was equally far to the Right, and although he was without the benefit of the many studies which had enriched the evenings of his shipmate, he was lively in debate, bitter in wit. He, too, was dark, but personable, with blue eyes and a dulcet brogue, and he uttered his doubts of the Left with soft dissenting vowels of a peasant out of Synge. The third of the trio who, in turn, occupied the wireless cabin was a quiet, studious creature from Warwickshire. He was so reticent that we were often persuaded that we had but two 'Sparks' on board, yet Aston was efficient, even more efficient than the others. When he came to the bridge or to the Captain's cabin he seemed always a hesitant, nervous creature. Later he became an applicant for a commission and we learned he had been at Rugby and for one year at Cambridge, and was by way of being a scientist, but he had broken his University course and had volunteered for the Navy.

The 'Bunts' were not so violently opposed in character. All three came from London. The only subject which gave them argument, but that hotly and often, was a belief shared between two of them that the River Thames imposed differences of outlook upon those who lived north or south of its ancient course. Mitchell, small, quick-tongued, quick-tempered, came from Brixton; Nichols, taller, slower, almost contemplative, from Finsbury Park. Once, after listening to their argument, I asked whether Leicester Square contained more of the north than the south in its character, but Nichols said that the differences of character of which he spoke were apparent only 'where people lived'. 'In residential areas,' he added authoritatively. Mitchell almost agreed, but then stipulated that Mitcham Fair was quite different in character from Hampstead Fair; less rowdy by far, he said. He kept to his belief, prepared to give Leicester Square to the northerners if London's Sassenachs might retain their Mitcham Fair unsullied. I think that these are perhaps widely held beliefs amongst Londoners, and it was amusing to hear the two protagonists engaged upon the question upon the bridge of *Tobias*.

Their companion was a small, white-faced, red-nosed ex-clerk from a printing-house. Hargreaves had no time for badinage. All his time off watch was spent in writing to his wife. During the first week on board he wrote three letters which Richmond was required to censor before leaving Halifax: the first was thirty pages long, the second sixteen and the third twenty.

'He seems unromantic in appearance,' said Richmond in the wardroom, 'but I can assure you he has some very romantic turns of phrase.'

'I take it he loves her dearly,' said Benson. 'Does he ever introduce the subject of sex?'

'In a roundabout sort of way. He is really quite a Shelley.'

'Shelley drowned, didn't he?' said the Captain. Sometimes his remarks were depressing.

❧

We were nine days out, almost half-way across, and breathed more evenly.

'At any time after midnight tonight,' said Benson, reappearing from under the chart table curtain, 'I estimate that we shall have rather less than fourteen hundred miles to row, either west or east.'

'You are very comforting, Alphabet,' said the Captain. 'Are you any good as a wet-bob?'

'There have been many notable oars in my family, sir.'

'That is to be considered a joke, I suppose?'

'It was not considered so in the family, sir.'

'Let's have some coffee, then, and then let's hear some more about your peculiar relations.'

Coffee came, rich, thick, but drinkable. In that at least, I had moved on from life in *Solander*, for in *Tobias* I had made an oligarchic decision that in the first, middle and morning watches only coffee would be drunk. This I had done from the first day, without consultation with the others, and coffee came to the bridge in these hours and all were satisfied. On one bridge, at least, of His Majesty's Navy, the immutable dynasty of galley tea had been overthrown and at last I was able to drink when others drank. No longer was my squeamish stomach made more squeamish by the sight of dixeys or mugs of thick brown brew. They could drink these potions in the day, but at night coffee only could be had.

We drank, mused upon the convoy, on our chances of getting through without a loss and returned to the vagaries of Benson's family tree, a subject which gave him much scope and ourselves much mirth. We had quickly slipped into the habit of yarning in the last half-hour of the first watch. In reasonable weather I usually climbed to the bridge about half an hour before midnight to relieve Willoughby. Benson was understudying the Captain, serving his watchkeeping apprenticeship during the first and forenoon watches. Richmond came up later at midnight, his appointed hour of relief, to join me.

Benson was being exceedingly eloquent upon his family's failings when, at 2353 hours, a ship was sunk.

At 2355 another.

At 2357 a third.

Across the convoy the explosions came as dull thuds. The first ship flared immediately.

'Tanker,' said Willoughby. 'Poor bastards!'

The bell was gonging 'Action Stations' through the ship. Men closed about the forward gun, moving from hunched silhouettes into living creatures, alert and chattering. The ship was nervously alive. In my stomach I felt again that sickness inseparable from fear, an inevitable prelude to action. Going down the ladder I had a momentary thought for the men in the tanker, wondering how they were faring in this always-expected hell, always so unexpected in its coming. I moved quickly along the deck, going aft. The depth charge crews were already closed up, stamping their feet upon the wooden deck amidships, the iron plates aft. They seemed unemotional, unperturbed, incurious, still sleepy. For them it was interruption to slumber.

'We may have work,' I said.

'Aye, aye, sir. Jerry about, sir?'

'He's just tinfished three ships.'

'Has he the noo, the bastard,' a Scot's voice said.

I moved round from the port to the starboard throwers. Two muffled figures chatted together as if waiting for a practice firing. 'Jerry about, sir?' one called, and, hearing my news, looked again to his pistols and his settings, his blue flashlight pressed close against the canister, his great duffel coat shielding the faint ray.

Forward, at the four-inch gun, Richmond was closed up with his crew. I voiced a hope that he might get a chance to use his ballistics.

'Hope so, Number One. Would be rather exciting.'

I thought his crew would agree and climbed once more to the bridge.

Willoughby was outside the bridge-house, looking across the sea to the blazing tanker. He moved within as I came up.

'That's the only one I can still see,' he said. 'There was a flash from one of the others, but she's gone or they've got the fire under control. Think the third one must have gone.'

I wondered aloud whether the tanker had had two of the torpedoes.

'Too long an interval for the one attack, I think. Full two minutes. I saw explosions in three different places over on that port wing. Think we've probably run into a pack.'

I thought so, too: it was evasion and pretence to hope that my theory might have truth in it.

'Keep a lookout for lifeboats,' he megaphoned to lookouts. 'And you, too, gun's crew.'

'Aye, aye, sir,' voices came thinly to the bridge. The wind seemed to be getting up or perhaps I was more suddenly aware of its wail.

We moved on the starboard beam of the convoy. Darkness hid the shambles from us. Only the tanker blazed. Around us, far to port, we knew that ships were driving into the night upon the prearranged course of their attempted escape, if attacks should come. We moved from our set course to the northward.

'Might as well try to shield this part of the convoy,' said Willoughby. Mason, the leading asdic rating, said, 'Ping, sir!' in a sudden voice which burst within the bridge-house like a paper bag.

We turned to him and watched the beginning of the hunt recorded upon the face of the asdic clock. The operator was bent to his task, crouched more tautly within the iron cabinet which enclosed him and his machine. A small yellow light lit him fitfully and in strange relief so that he looked like a symbol of mechanical warfare drawn perhaps by Mr Henry Moore. His head was still, but his shoulders moved slowly down as if weighed, and his hand at the instrument sharply showed the knuckles, bony and white. Benson stood over him, tense, held like a figure struck in metal. I wished that I could follow the pattern of the hunt as easily as he. His round, bland face was set in harsh concentration. I looked to Willoughby; he glanced to the sea and back to Benson and to Mason. One hand held limply to the strap of his binoculars, slung about his neck. The glasses he did not use. His other hand gripped the rail built around the inside of the bridge-house. He muttered, but I heard no words. The decreasing hum of the asdic echoes came to my ears, singing in sharp, urgent notes as they held to the enemy. The windows of the bridge-house were down;

Willoughby called to Ross, smothered and unrecognisable in his great duffel coat.

'Call up the senior escort, Ross!'

'Aye, aye, sir,' said Ross, but in the wind's high voice his words were lost; I saw only movements of his lips.

The destroyer was away on our port bow. Willoughby, shouting the words into Sparks's ears, gave his message: 'Think–I–have–contact.'

The wind caught his words away as they were yelled, but the flashes went out at a speed I could not follow, and were accepted. The reply was immediate. Sparks moved steeply aft along the sloping bridge to crouch to take the message. 'Joining-you.' I saw other aldis flashes from the port side of the destroyer. 'Probably getting another escort in the hunt,' said Willoughby, and turned again to the asdic cabinet. The echo still held. Mason lost it momentarily, and I smiled to see the sudden panic on his face, and wondered whether he was fearful of Willoughby's cold words or of his own condemning conscience.

The night still held many clouds, and sudden rain squalls. The shapes of the few ships near *Tobias* were vague, almost lost in overhanging darkness; but sometimes clouds, over-racing each other, gave sudden breaks, and ships were bolder to our eyes. No orders had yet come to them to disperse. They continued in company upon a new course as if unaware of the enemies about and amongst them. Yet I knew that already rumour would be abroad within each ship. Masters and men would be watching the signals across the convoy with straining, speculative eyes, waiting for the order that they should be once more upon their own.

In such moments the casual, social, talkative life of a ship is wholly altered. Few calls or whispers live between the members of the crew. Men seem to slip swiftly into their own thoughts and to become, on the instant, remote from their fellows. They would act together as a crew, and obey all orders with precision; yet they were obviously preoccupied, thinking. This was so in *Tobias*. I watched the lookouts on the bridge staring more intently into the night than they had stared before in their brief life upon the Atlantic. They scarcely heeded the voice of the Captain calling to Sparks. They were alert and ready for action. I wondered what their thoughts might be, but this is an abiding curiosity, and could not stay me from going below and groping my way aft to the depth charge stations, at Willoughby's order that I should have 'another look-see aft'.

I returned to the port thrower. The two men were quiet, staring at the sea, clinging to the thrower as the corvette climbed the sea's sharp sides and fell. I went on, tripping over a fender which had broken from its hold. I clewed it up again and groped an undignified way to the chutes. I remembered my own weary vigils on such nights in the stern of *Solander*, and was at one with the leading hand in his wish for reassurance upon the priming and setting he had given to the charges.

I asked my routine questions, verified that settings were correct, turned and clambered forward again, climbed to the bandstand. The pom-pom crew was closed up; the spotter looked glumly over the platform's edge, yelled 'Does it look like business, sir?' and clapped his mittened hands together at my reply that we had got a ping.

'I read once they usually come up through the conning tower if they do come up to fight it out; that's right, ain't it, sir?' He yelled his question three times as I clung to the ladder, the wind catching his words away like spume, sending its idiocy flying to the south. I wondered how he thought a U-boat's crew would appear, but forbore to check enthusiasm by such acerbic comment, and went down the rungs and moved once more to the starboard thrower. Both men were stamping upon the iron plates; they had turned out too lightly clad for the night. They would learn this way, I thought; even though they affected to consider their chill a matter of no moment. Next time I should find them as snugly clad against the night as polar bears. I climbed again to the bridge. The echoes had been lost; Benson was livid, blasphemous; Willoughby was quiet. 'Probably a shoal of fish,' Benson said, 'but Mason swears it's metal he's been hitting and he knows his stuff', and he swore foully.

Mason was working urgently upon his dial. 'Perhaps I brought that damned destroyer over too soon,' said Willoughby, almost musing. 'I'll get a bottle if I have.'

'Got it again, sir!' said Mason, and once more we saw upon the asdic dial the record of the thing we sought.

Willoughby gave his orders to the helmsman, swiftly, urgently. I looked to the destroyer and saw that she too must have the echo. An old W Class destroyer was also joining in the hunt. They were blurred outlines in the darkness. Their purpose was apparent. They would sow their patterns with *Tobias*. The three ships would now work as a team and Willoughby would take his orders from the senior escort.

Flashes from the destroyer gave us directions. We would try to hold our echoes and keep a fix upon the enemy. The three ships would move into the first attack upon their present courses. *Tobias* would sow the final pattern.

'That suits me,' said Willoughby.

Dawn lay most faintly upon the edge of the ocean as we went in. The Captain steadied the ship on her course, brought her up to full speed and we went in to attack. Mason was as immobile as any component of his apparatus, as if he had been fused into its unity. The two destroyers steamed towards each other, moving as if they must collide. I had watched and taken part in this drill often enough during anti-submarine training, and in action in *Solander*, but now I could not believe that the drill could work, smoothly, efficiently.

Tobias would attack a few seconds after the old W destroyer had sown its pattern. Our slower speed, compared with the destroyers', might make the manoeuvre somewhat complicated when we came round for the second 'run in'. The thought was also in the Captain's mind, for he said, 'This is going to be slightly tricky, Number One. I'd give a lot for another five knots!'

Spouts came up from the senior escort's charges, as they exploded deep in the ocean. In the dim light they were momentary swirls against a darker background, the spouts rising swiftly and falling in blurred cascades. The explosions from the W destroyer followed. Then we were in again.

We were still getting echoes.

'The blighter's tricky,' said Willoughby. 'He's gone pretty deep and going deeper. Hold him, Mason. Jump to it, Sparks, the destroyer's calling up.'

Sparks spelled out the simple message: 'Rejoin convoy.'

'My God!' said Willoughby. For a moment his language was unprintable. '... and to think that I brought those men into the picture!'

We went round on a 200 degree turn. The two destroyers would continue the hunt. They were edging away from the position of our last attack, coming round again for another run in.

'God, oh God, oh God,' moaned Willoughby. We were all angered and quiet. A few minutes later Willoughby said: 'It was really jolly decent of the destroyers to let us have one attack – with the convoy to think of. I knew that order would come, but hoped it wouldn't. Oh God, what luck.'

We moved steadily upon our course to the north. We were quiet for a long, long time. At last the dawn grew greyly upon us, lifting slowly like a pale curtain after a play of macabre intent. Far to the north were the specks of the convoys.

'They'll certainly need all the escorts they can get if any of those so-and-so's are still about,' said Benson, and with that assertion we all agreed.

Between dawn and eight o'clock the convoy was mustered again and we proceeded once more upon our prearranged zig-zags, working more to the north than in our earlier routeing. At nine o'clock the two destroyers rejoined the convoy. The following half-hour Willoughby considered to be the most galling period in his whole life, for, after an exchange of signals, we learned that a U-boat had been sunk in their attack and five prisoners taken.

'Our U-boat!' he cried aloud, and could not be comforted, and in this lively use of the collective pronoun he engaged us all as partners in the curses he called down upon all destroyers and all destroyer captains in the Royal Navy.

❧

During that day our conversation was a lament on our lost U-boat and preoccupation with the sloth of our charges. At teatime Richmond often examined these questions of the war at sea in its relation to the lives of men. Most of us accepted the inescapable fact that we were sailors, that we served in ships, that we had certain jobs to do. The cold logistics whereby ships were moved upon the ocean, and men were moved to certain ships for certain jobs did not enter much into our lives. Sometimes we railed, but usually we were too busy eating, sleeping, watchkeeping, and it is certain that although the men might grumble at many aspects of their lives, they, too, were kept too busy eating, sleeping, working.

I sat with Richmond in the wardroom during the first dog watch. We sipped at tea and he cut into a plum cake made by Jake's fair hands.

'What is the average speed of this convoy, Number One?'

'About seven knots – if we're lucky.'

'How many of these merchantmen have been built since the war?'

'None, I should say.'

'Doesn't it seem incredible to you, that our rulers have watched the progress of the U-boat since the last war and have done absolutely nothing to increase the speed of our merchant ships in all the years of peace?'

I suggested that our rulers, like the rest of us, did not expect war.

'As a seafaring nation we have no right to live if we are not always prepared for war, at least, at sea, and here we are with a typical convoy of this war that's no faster than a similar convoy of the last war, and U-boats, I should say, have added at least three knots to their submerged speeds and probably five knots to their surface speed.'

'We are all to blame,' I said. 'If a nation has the government it deserves it usually has the armed forces it deserves.'

Richmond was determined to keep to facts.

'If all the merchantmen in this convoy could make fifteen knots, how many ships d'you think we'd have lost last night?'

I had thought too often upon that subject to delay my answer, and said, 'Probably none.'

'Then why haven't we been building fifteen-knot merchantmen for the past ten years?'

'They're uneconomical to run, I'm told.'

'Now they're unwarlike.'

Richmond brooded dolorously upon these facts. When I might deal more realistically, less imaginatively, with the actuality of a seven-knot convoy he was caught away into frustrating examination of what might have been had we been a nation of farsighted seafarers. I could see with him and agree with his denunciations, but I am not made of this crusading stuff; the white heat of conviction and devils of idealism do not burn uncivilly within me, yet I record our conversation, for there is much truth in all that Richmond said. As I recall his bitter words, I hear again his pleasant, gentle voice, trying to remain calm in his subject as he remembered the flaming tanker, remembered too, the strange neglect of many shipowners who would build slow ships for inexpensive peacetime trading and then expect, as if by miracle, these same ungainly freighters to cross the ocean in times of total war.

'They still expect their profits, I suppose,' said Richmond. 'I don't suppose they let the government have 'em at cost price. It's just up to the ingenuity of the routeing people at home, the gameness of these RN commodores, the bravery of these merchant navy types and the work of thousands of willing fools like you and me.'

'You have all truth with you, Rich,' I said. 'Yet reality eludes you. We escort these wheezing merchantmen. We shall probably lose more ships tonight. We must work with what we have. We are all to blame. All the things you say are wishes and all your theories hopes. It has all happened before and I think it may all happen again, and I must go and relieve Willoughby who likes his tea.'

'If I thought like you I should slit my throat,' said Richmond, as I reached for my duffel coat.

'And if I thought like you I should go into politics.'

Richmond said that he preferred architecture.

'Which is another way of saying you'll leave the shipowners to do it all over again.'

'We shall see,' said Richmond. 'What beats me is how you can remain so unperturbed.'

I was deeply perturbed, I admitted, but I had been born a pessimist, he an idealist, and in these moments the contrast of those origins was suddenly apparent.

'Bah!' he said, and smiled, but ruefully.

That night we lost two more vessels. On the following day, the eleventh of the passage, we were in no mood to discuss any abstractions related to the philosophy of shipowning. Between the hours of seven at night and seven in the morning no man slept. Thus sleep was apportioned between the watches of the day. We were tired beyond the normal sense of tiredness. Willoughby had slept for three hours in fifty and moved about the bridge like a taut animal, his face gaunt, his eyes most strained but in temper controlled. The two junior officers slept fitfully watch and watch under Willoughby's insistence. I slept for short periods in the wooden bunk in the bridge-house. Willoughby borrowed this monastic berth for short periods, but did not sleep, I noticed, staring instead at the asdic operator or to the clouds moving beyond the windows, seeming to brood upon the destiny of the convoy as if he were its commodore.

During the day the destroyers worked far astern, patrolling, searching. Sometimes we heard faintly the explosion of depth charges, but mainly they were, we judged, about eight miles off, seeking to drive the U-boats deep, to slow them down so that the possible periods of attack during the coming night would be shortened by hours or even minutes. At dusk they came up astern of the convoy, the senior ship flashing brief messages concerning station-keeping, and then both returned to their vigil astern, from where the attacks would most likely come. Yet the U-boats, we knew, often left the convoys far to the north and proceeded, surfaced, at a greater speed than we could make, to lay athwart our course at dusk or at dawn. Then they could most easily and most accurately make their attacks.

For us there was no certainty of place or time for their attacks. As dusk fell like a heavy mist about the shapes of ships we settled once more to a slow, minute-by-minute staring into the night and a continuous, nervous, over-the-shoulder consideration of the asdic dial. The strain was intense, chiselling minutely at patience and sanity through the long hours of the night.

Attacks always came suddenly although always expected. The shock of that suddenness was made more emphatic by reason of our waiting. We closed in upon the convoy to pick up survivors and to hunt the attackers. There was a melee and men came alongside and were pulled on board. The night was crowded, hideous and over everything was the gloom of the ocean night which could not be lightened if we wished to live.

~&

The third night we lost two more ships.

~&

After that we lost no more. During the following day we were within range of the Sunderlands of Coastal Command. We could not believe that we should not have these nightmares again for at least a week. Relief was boundless, worth an alleluia from more devout mariners, but instead, more soberly, we stared at the lovely hills of Donegal, trying to pierce the mists to seize the sight of what we might persuade ourselves was Errigail, and then was Malin Head and then Loch Foyle.

'We leave them here,' said Willoughby, 'for officially, Number One, although recent experiences might persuade you to think otherwise, we are not yet considered in all respects ready for war'; but I was staring too fondly at the kindly Irish hills to wish to think of the war at sea.

Chapter 5

Sailors in a Lunar Landscape

Off the northern Irish coast we passed a week in 'working-up'. Anti-submarine exercises, gunnery trials, tests in seamanship, mock depth charge attacks occupied all our days and in the evenings we were too tired to go ashore. We had pleasant dinners in the wardroom, talked over the day, discussed any theories which might have been introduced into conversation during the meal and then parted, to read, to smoke, or to sleep. Each evening I wrote two or three letters, read part of Mr Maugham's *Cakes and Ale,* and then slept, switching off my lamp at ten o'clock, glad that Richmond and Benson were duty officers and that until six in the morning I would forget and be forgotten.

❧

A long letter came from Hilary Hughes, shipmate and companion of *Solander,* answering many questions. His letter left me with no doubts that he was enjoying life in his new ship, although he was not, it appeared, very keen on the tropics. It was interesting, too, to hear what was happening to other mariners steaming many hundreds of miles to the south in a less steep Atlantic stream. 'As usual,' he began, 'I suppose you are thinking me a pretty average sort of twerp for not writing, but I have the usual excuse that quite a lot has been happening to me since I left the old ship. I was terribly sorry to leave old Dickens, Broughton and yourself but I quite like the idea of being a Jimmy and I had a hankering for sun. My God, did I get it! But first things first. I went home on my forty-eight hours' leave to say goodbye to the family. We sailed a day or two later. Usual naval fashion. Hell of a flap for no reason at all. Since being out here we've done sweet Fanny Adams.' He then proceeded to a gloomy account of life in Freetown and Lagos. 'Here we swelter and sweat in godawful heat. What wouldn't I give for a good pea-soup fog again! And everyone thinks you're a sissy if you don't have a bout of malaria every fortnight ...' and so on, in self-appreciating gloom. In superstition I touched the wooden drawer of my cabin desk, hoping that I should keep to the north and with many chances to look beyond the scuttles to the Ulster hills.

❧

For a while we kept to the north, for we were put on the Iceland run. This knowledge was relief to forebodings that we might find ourselves upon the old *Solander* run: across the Atlantic with one convoy and back with another, and scarcely the sight of a land other than our own. In concert with most other sailors, I thought that war might prove more bearable with the chance of seeing lands and peoples I had not seen before, the cost to be borne mainly by His Britannic Majesty's Government. This was perhaps a miserly, unpatriotic view of the war, but one yet fashionably established amongst the officers and crews of the Royal Navy. I had, too, much curiosity concerning the northern lands. In times of peace I had travelled in all the countries of Scandinavia, and now looked forward to seeing, for the first time, this outpost of those lands, for it was in such a manner that I regarded this island of saga, lava, deserts, volcanoes and an ancient people to which we were now directed.

The Captain thought in other ways. 'It is sure to be cold,' he said. 'The food will be awful and the women ill-clad and uninviting. It is always so in the northern world.' I smiled to hear such fastidious lament, but he continued, brooding upon the malevolent fate which kept him from the Med.

The 'run' became a frequent pleasure throughout that early summer. We made four journeys to Reykjavik, and I came to know something of its way of life, especially as Willoughby lacked all desire to go ashore, insisting that I should pay all possible political and duty calls to the office of the NOIC, or Naval-Officer-in-Charge of the base. In the evenings he had his parties on board or scribbled occasional postcards to those he termed his 'well-connected fleshpot friends in the City and the County', and always with his words he smiled and turned once more to the ship's gin for another noggin. His parties, however, were his main delight; he enjoyed to the full the delicate task of their arrangement. His invitations were always neatly typewritten upon small cards and sent across to other ships to be delivered by a leading hand from one of the lifeboats. The Captain said that such formality gave the boat's crew needed practice in the handling of their craft, gave the ship a certain prestige about the port, and gave his parties 'a dignity in their invitations which might be lacking in their farewells'. These morning invitations became of repute amongst the ships when we were in harbour, and

'Away party boat!' became a smirking, whispered catcall on the lower deck; but the Captain smiled.

We were a truly happy ship all through that summer. Under Willoughby's sardonic but genial autocracy we could never be unhappy for long, but the prospect of the short run and continuing good weather put the crew to merry moods. They were also shaking down to their jobs, and with increasing mastery of appointed tasks, men become light-hearted, despite their growls and discontent. I came to delight in the routine of the run, noting also in myself less hesitancy in movement and in orders, becoming, too, less chary to make decisions and in giving orders under the amused and searching eyes of Willoughby. I was getting to know a few members of the crew. Jake Gibbs, the wardroom steward, had already shown us whilst in Canada that his was a bizarre personality. He was a short, thick-set man of twenty-five with hulking shoulders, barrel chest and bowed legs. Between meals he moved about the wardroom attired in a grimy white sweater and dungaree slacks. His sweater was a proud possession, for he had been a submariner for six months and would not let any of the crew forget that this had been a truly hazardous experience. Although he had a round, flabby, unhealthy face, he was strong beyond the limit of any other man in the ship and was useful outside the wardroom, especially when a strong hand was needed at the hawsers aft. He gloried in this appalling strength, and when one of the officers was alone in the wardroom, Gibbs' tales of his moments of peacetime triumphs in all-in wrestling bouts at Blackfriars Ring and at Lanes in Baker Street were certain to be told with bright eyes, unholy relish and gory detail. Benson quickly memorised many of these recitals, realising their value in his repertory, and he would shatter moments of silence on the bridge with sudden intrusions: 'so I 'ad 'im down, see, sir, down on 'is back, flat as a bleedin' pancake. I'm squattin' across his guts, me arse well into 'is you know what, sir. I gets both 'is arms pinioned and then I raises 'em and brings 'is elbows dahn crack on the deck, see, sir. Then again. And again. The whole 'ouse is 'ollering ...' So good a mimic was Alphabet that we were immediately chuckling. 'If Gibbs ever hears your take-off, Benson,' said the Captain, 'you'll have him squattin' across your guts, sitting well into your you know what. Not that I'd be greatly perturbed, but he's too good a steward to put on to any other job.'

He was indeed a good steward, tending us with kindliness and precision. Meals were never late: at all times coffee was ready for watchkeeping officers; at any time he could produce a cup of China tea fit to offer to a party from ashore. He had also much skill as a pastry-cook and many afternoons were made glorious in our memories by fruit cake or treacle sponge made by Jake Gibbs, 'I just knocked it up while cook got his head down, sir. Picked up the recipe from me old woman.'

King, the depth charge rating, was another character (how quickly the stronger and livelier personalities emerged amongst the crew!). He was crafty, cunning, lecherous, low in mind and character, and likeable. He could do a job more quickly than anyone on board, from getting a whaler ship-shape to a peculiarly difficult piece of wire splicing, yet he was bone lazy. He would finish his task in impeccable style and then disappear to get his head down. He was a tall, dark, brazen, handsome London lout, with always a trace of a moustache within two hours of shaving. He swaggered when walking ashore and carried a mental swagger into all his conversations on board. He was a wit amongst the crew, yet apart from them, for it was clear that he considered them sheep, dull and slow in thought. He was a long-service rating and had been mentioned in despatches in the Norwegian campaign; twice he had been advanced to leading hand, his record said, and twice had reverted to ordinary seaman.

Now once more he was leading hand, but it was an uneasy elevation. I spoke to him one evening whilst checking the depth charge settings, asking whether he liked his job.

'Yes. Think I do, sir.'

'Will you stay leading hand, then?' (for he knew I had his record).

'Always a bit of a problem, sir.'

'Why?'

'I get on the booze, overstay me leave, then cells and down I go again.'

'Sounds crazy to me.'

'Sounds crazy to me, sir. Women, sir. Can't keep away from 'em.'

His bland admissions were always lacking in normal anglican hypocrisy and therefore somewhat surprising.

'Ever tried marriage?' (I knew he was married from Richmond's having mentioned that he had censored a rather lurid letter from King to his wife.)

'Yessir, tried that, but I could tackle a dozen wives. Easy meat. She's all right. I shoulda been a sultan or something.'

I wondered whether the vagaries of such conversation between officer and man were allowed for in *KR & AI*.

'Pity if you go down again. The Captain takes a poor view of it.'

'Can see 'is point of view, sir.'

'How old are you?'

'Twenty-four, sir.'

'You're a mug, King. You could be Acting PO in a couple of years if you pulled your socks up. What setting d'you give that third charge?'

'Two-fifty feet, sir.'

I wondered whether we might make something of him: King had made it clear that it was a difficult task.

One or other of the communications ratings – visual signals – was always with us on the bridge, and the personalities of Mitchell and Nichols became a perennially pleasant clash as they relieved each other. Hargreaves kept always to his own thoughts and possibly romantic yearnings for his home and wife.

Benson controlled the lives of the asdic ratings, and these I saw but slightly, and then only upon matters of routine and discipline. I saw even less of the Chief Mechanics, ERAs – Engine Room Artificers – and the stokers from the engine-room.

Occasionally upon some question of pay or possible advancement they came to my cabin, but they came almost solely under the care of Warrant Officer Dundass and to him, I knew, their fates and lives were justly entrusted: he would know every Service answer to every Service query, as I quickly learned, for to him I often went with the trickier questions of my own job and from him always received simple, swift elucidation, for few naval problems could long prevail against his many years of the lower-deck and now the wardroom. His answers, after sober deliberation, were given ponderous utterance, judicial, unassailable. He knew *KR & AI* as if it had been his only reading from boyhood, as perhaps it had. Upon questions of discipline and courtesies, pay and allowances he was a Fleet oracle, and later, as we came to have some understanding of the full depth of naval lore and law he contained within his vast, sand-coloured cranium, we were inclined, I sometimes thought, to overtax his indulgence of our curiosity, yet perhaps not. He seemed to like the role and few men in this world object to a lay audience for their voices and their learning.

The three Chief Petty Officers: the Coxswain, Reynolds; 'Guns' Campbell; and Tugwell, the engine-room deputy to Dundass, were long-service men with impressive records.

At all times their advice was invoked and always they responded.

❧

Thus, with growing understanding of ourselves, our crew, and occasionally of our strangely assorted, and often ancient, fleets of merchantmen, that uncharitable gap of ocean, the beat of the Northern Patrol, became almost a task of pleasure during that summer, and when the look-out called that land was sighted on the starboard bow, and I knew that once more we were coming to the Westmann Islands, I could have rubbed my mittened hands in pleasure (and sometimes did).

The first time was an experience of wonder. We sighted the Islands far off to starboard about midday and came up to the mainland in the early afternoon. Even in high summer the coastline was bleak, the mountains misted and snowsloped. I kept to the glasses, fascinated by the desolate, almost macabre landscape. Those qualities were enhanced by the glasses which will often invest a landscape, or a ship in a seascape, with many attributes of toys; and now it was as if we had journeyed to a model of the moon. The earth seemed pitted, scorched and wholly lunar in its desolation. The harsh coastline, with the thin thread of the tide, advancing and receding against minute stretches of beach or against dark rocks, seemed far-off, not of this world. Even the waves appeared toylike and slow-moving.

From the chart and the *Iceland and Faroes Pilot* I knew that the rocks to the north, edging out into the Atlantic, hid the long wedges which the fiords drove far into the land. Inland were the ridges of mountains, as ragged as the recordings of a seismograph in a time of hectic movement. These mountains were quite unlike the slowly climbing hills of Wales I knew so well, or the sudden emergence of great summits in the Alps. I held to the glasses, my eyes staring and untiring.

Thus we crept, in company with our valuable charges, around the south-western tip of the island, past the small fishing village of Hafnafjordur, which was to become a destination for future excursions across the lava fields in the local afternoon bus from Reykjavik. The small, gaily painted houses were upon our beam, recalling with their blues, pinks and whites, the Norwegian fishing villages I had seen during the previous year from the deck of the trawler, *Alaskan*.

The first afternoon I went ashore with Willoughby. He had to report to the NOIC, and I wished to see the 'chips' at the base, for we had several of those odd jobs which inevitably arise about the mess-decks during each voyage and need expert attention. I also had to see about our water supply, for the tanks seemed to have been too well impregnated against infection, and we wished to know whether it was the water, its chlorination, or the lining of the tanks which brought such unsavoury drinks to our meals. We had suspected this on our maiden voyage, but the evidence had not been sure. Now, it seemed, proof came with time: within a week our water would be undrinkable, except as medicine. I talked of these requirements with the Captain. 'Good,' he said, 'get them done'; he would return to sleep; the sightseer could look around. I smiled and went, fixing appointments with experts from the base for early the following morning on board *Tobias*. Afterwards I wandered about the town.

⟶❧

Reykjavik at that time was rather like a gold-rush town which had convinced itself, or had been convinced by its civic leaders, that it ought not to lose interest in the cultural side of things. Consequently the town held unconventional contradictions: in the centre of the town were streets as pot-holed, rutted and acutely cambered, as unkempt Irish lanes; yet there were several modern, well-designed warehouses by the quays. There was an impressive university building in the contemporary manner, built from the proceeds of a public lottery, just outside the town (even this university building was set back some distance from a most inferior road), but many filthy restaurants and eating houses. There were public hot baths, super Chrysler and Buick taxis, a few pretentious hotels and several squalid roaming-houses, two antique cinemas, and chromium-and-glass ice cream parlours. All these contrasts can be found in any capital, but in Reykjavik they were concentrated into a comparatively small area and contrasts were sharp to the eyes.

The domestic architecture of the town was equally pleasing and depressing in emphatic contrast. Skilful use had been made of corrugated iron throughout the town. Six or seven out of every ten houses seemed to be constructed from this unsympathetic material, yet, by the cunning and decorative use of bright colours, the general effect had charm. Seen from the bridge of *Tobias* these colours had given an impression that Reykjavik was a pleasantly timbered and painted town in the Norwegian tradition, but there are so few trees on the island that it would be almost impossible to erect timbered houses in any number. (Many months later, in Brisbane, I was to see how less cunningly corrugated iron could be used, for in that city almost all roofs are built in this material, and, by a ubiquitous use of fawns and dark reds, the city seems dull and lifeless under its sub-tropical sun.)

The Scandinavian tradition was, however, frequently apparent in Reykjavik. The corrugated iron sheeting had been cut into strange shapes and patterns in order to achieve the authentic steeply-pitched roofs and fulsome eaves: the results were often pleasing. I walked around one of the residential areas, the *Tungata*. Greys and blues were here successfully used, and from their exteriors I judged the houses comfortable to live in. To one arriving from England, this part of the town had a serenity which I had almost forgotten could be the evening quality of a town, although I supposed that serenity was still known in Winchester or Chichester and a hundred other towns in Britain. Londoners are too often prone to believe the Great Wen to be Great Britain!

At the other end of the architectural scale were the slums. I came across these in a journey I made for the Captain on the second day of our stay. He had a note of introduction to a major who was based 'somewhere in Iceland'. Willoughby thought that it would be a splendid idea to invite a couple of soldiers to a party he was preparing for the following evening. I was going ashore to the base; he thought I might try to track the major down. I pointed out that Iceland was two-thirds the size of Ireland, and, therefore, a fair-sized place in which to look for a major, but he handed me a flimsy sheet of notepaper with the usual hieroglyphics representing a military unit. The fact that the chap was a sapper ought to help, said Willoughby, and, with one of his casual grins, he turned towards his cabin and left me, one foot irresolute upon the rope ladder.

I took the tiller and was pulled ashore. Seated in the bobbing boat, I was preoccupied with this task and its demonstration of the personality of my Captain. How often I had heard it said that it was imperative that a First Lieutenant should know something of the mind and manners of his Captain; that too often a lack of understanding was responsible for the beginning of flaws between these two vital links in the life of the ship; tension grew, the links snapped with sudden damage. I had, even in my brief naval career, heard and seen several instances of that, but, perhaps complacently, thought there was little chance of such misunderstandings arising between

Willoughby and myself; our personalities were reasonably complementary, and I was beginning to understand the way his mind worked. His seeming casualness fooled nobody, certainly not the crew. At sea, or in harbour, he might wander out from his cabin after breakfast, regarding the sky as blandly and innocently as a clergyman on a south-coast promenade, but the men on watch knew that stare by now, and I always smiled to see their furtive movements and glances along the deck to see what was amiss. Willoughby's gentle inquiry, 'Robinson, did you stow that wire?' or, 'Healy, why is that fender loose?' was often the prelude to an equally gentle but incisive 'bottle' for unseamanlike ways and general remissness. I felt my own responsibilities in these matters and did my best to get everything shipshape, but Willoughby's faraway look invariably spotted some disturbing feature in the ship. (A skipper usually can when he desires.) Such precision might have become a nerve-wearing routine in other circumstances and under another Captain, but it was impossible that this could enter into any dealings between Willoughby and his officers and men. His inquiries had no psychological complex for their background, unless a preoccupation with neatness is a complex. He was quite unlike my former Captain: Dickens had been simple and direct, with outbursts of temper that were like sudden squalls about the ship, but Willoughby was devious in his approach to the crew, and never lost his temper, preserving rather a calm and genial interest in a culprit and his misdeed. He asked his questions as if he were making a nominal inspection, 'just like he was askin'' if your old woman was expecting twins,' I once overheard one of the 'killicks' say, but the deadliness of his innocent approach had them on their toes from the beginning of the ship's life. The crew of *Solander* had respected Dickens because they respected his efficiency and understood him; the crew of *Tobias* respected Willoughby because they recognised his efficiency yet could

115

never understand him. They could understand a man who stormed at them and then subsided; they could not understand the icy detachment of Willoughby. Yet they liked him in their own way. They knew his worth, and, because there is cruelty in much English humour, his sardonic words appealed to them, even though they might often be the victims. His 'cracks', as they called his bitter slants at ineptitude, were remembered and included in letters home. ('The old man of this packet give me a dressing down yesterday for coming back from shore leave with me not looking like a tailor's dummy,' quoted Richmond from a letter home. The Captain, listening, smiled.) The men sensed the kindliness beneath the detachment, they understood his strength and calmness, and they followed him willingly as a leader.

In the odd task he had given me and which I now brooded upon, I recognised the Willoughby touch. There was no reason why he should have given me the job. There was no reason why I should make more than a perfunctory inquiry at the base and return with the honest answer that 'nobody seems to know'. Yet I would do all I could, I knew, and Willoughby knew that too. He could have sent either of the juniors, but he knew that because I knew something of the ways of naval bases, I would bring him an answer if an answer were possible. With his casual, almost offhand charm he extracted the last degree of usefulness from his men. I saw myself and my present task as demonstration of that truth.

I collected the signals and chart corrections I wanted from various cubicles in the warrens of 'The Base', and went off to a room in an office building a hundred yards away. There, I was told by a signals officer, I should find the local representatives of the Division of Naval Intelligence 'living in wild abandon'. One of them might help me track down Willoughby's major.

I was lucky. One of the junior officers there was a lieutenant, RNVR, with whom I had been under training in *King Alfred*.

Lieutenant Manston said it was easy, rang up somebody he called 'old boy', then somebody else he called 'old man' and thus located the sapper. He then capped his man-hunt by offering to drive me out to the camp about ten miles away. 'I've got to see them about some local waterworks we're interested in, and you can look for your chap whilst I do my job,' he said, and grabbed his cap and went to find a taxi. I followed his wild, abandoned exit.

Taxis were obtained, Manston said, by going to one of the four or five taxi stations in the centre of the town and booking a cab. It just wasn't done to hail a taxi in the streets. Three large American saloon cars were waiting at the garage; these were the taxis and we climbed into a large black Buick. Engaging taxis was conducted on a basis of issuing IOU chits, carrying the authority of the Royal Navy, to the taxi firms. Most of the drivers knew a little English, Manston said, and, continuing with his brief Baedeker to the capital, explained that the taxis were mainly these high-powered American saloons which were driven with the audacity of the peacetime Parisian taxi-driver. I asked why they were such recent models. Manston smiled: a large consignment of the cars had been en route for Denmark just before the Hun walked into Scandinavia; the cars were put ashore at Reykjavik and here they were. The drivers appeared to be reckless, but their accident record was really very low, he said, as I hurtled from my seat into his lap.

We went out from the town along the Bankastraeti, a long, straight, depressing street leading to the open country. There were many sordid houses and the whole area was like a grim industrial slum in the north of England, although not so bad as slums I had seen in Newcastle, the Potteries and mining districts of the Midlands. The buildings were like small tenements. Life for a hard-up family in a tenement in Reykjavik in these cramped quarters during the long and harsh Icelandic winter must surely be very gloomy, I said, and Manston agreed, saying that he had seen some of them the previous winter and could imagine very little worse; personally he would rather live in a hut in a lava desert than in the appalling squalor of these northern slums.

We drove out into the hills beyond the capital. I began to see the army at work. Manston was a ready commentator, and began to talk about their lives, saying that he thought I would find my major a ready guest as most of the army officers and almost all the men were extremely bored. A rumour had stirred that the present garrison would be relieved after one year of service, 'but I believe it's all moonshine and a dreadful delusion,' he said. 'The idea of the old Ministry of War Transport taking all these pongos back to Blighty and bringing out another lot doesn't seem to have ring of truth to me. Some of the technicians, on the other hand, simply don't want to go back until they've finished their jobs. You may find your major one of those queer chaps. You know the old sapper line: mad, married or Methodist. Some of the survey people are the same way. Very odd. Take this chap I'm going out to see. He's a kingpin on water supply. He won't hear about going back. He says he's helping to bring the water supply here into line with that of most of the other capitals of Europe and that it's a task worthy of any engineer. By the time these chaps have finished it'll be a sight better than anything we've got back home.'

Looking to both sides of the road I saw groups of men, building tracks and roads, burrowing into the stark hillside, levelling the approach to a small concrete bridge, obviously recently built. Beyond the workers, like a small town, stretched the rows of Nissen huts with khaki washing hung out to dry on lines strung between the huts. Men stood in groups, talking, washing, shaving, laughing, and in odd corners behind the huts others were punting footballs about. To a soldier from the First World War, I thought, this army of occupation would have shown few signs of change from that which tried to bring the peace to Germany, and made the peace too peaceful.

Manston, following my eyes, said, 'They all work pretty hard. They make roads, build bridges, metal runways. They're tough and wiry. They grouse like the very devil, and bellyache for home. This country is bleak and inhospitable to them. It's only the odd troops and the officers who get hold of the local beauties. Most of them have no interest in mild exploration. They'd rather be back in Bethnal Green or the Yorkshire dales. The nature of Icelandic literature or the volcanic structure of their new home has no appeal for them, and I don't blame them. To them, it's a cold and lousy land, and there's always the dreary prospect of spending another winter here, and they'd rather be in the desert, I sometimes think, than in this place, for it can be hellish here in winter. Here we are!' and he pointed to a signpost which recorded in the best English manner that this was Poona Camp. As I got out Manston was giving instructions for the driver to wait. I wondered how he liked Iceland. He smiled. 'I rather like the country. I was by way of being an Icelandic student before the war – an offshoot of Germanic studies – and asked to come up here when I was at *KA*. First they sent me off to a trawler, but later must have remembered. Odd, isn't it? Not often the old Admiralty remembers one's dearly-bought qualifications. So, in a way, I'm lucky.'

I tracked down Major G Blake, OBE, RE, after a series of interrogations conducted at 100-yard intervals. He was working in a large Nissen hut, surrounded by a crowd of typing and clerking privates and corporals, brooding malevolently over a large plan of Reykjavik and its environs which covered a trestle table. I gave him my message and the note from Willoughby's friend. 'Delighted,' he said. 'And I can bring one other chap? That's very noble of you. Haven't had a good binge in a month.' He called across the hut to a Captain. 'Donald, care to come on a party?' And then to me, 'I suppose you've got plenty of the old Plymouth Rock?'

I nodded my head, and said 'Buckets', thinking that Willoughby would prefer me to act the part of the connoisseur, for he was extremely serious about his duties as a host, and unduly proud of his special gin fizz made from the coveted Plymouth Rock.

'Good. We'll be there. Time?'

I said 'nineteen hundred' in the best inter-Services manner, and added that we would have the ship's lifeboat at the quay at that time.

'Good. We'll look forward to that,' and he rubbed his hands in glee.

I went back to Manston, and invited him, too. He said he would be delighted to come. Willoughby, I thought, would think I was hitting the high spots, inviting people to *Tobias* parties. An hour later I mentioned the fact in the wardroom as casually as possible. The Captain roared with laughter. 'Listen to that, chaps. Number One's stepping out. Bringing people on board to a drinking party. Be smuggling women on board next.'

From the guffaws I gathered that this was considered to be funny.

⤙

This was the third of Willoughby's parties I had attended, but I was beginning to be persuaded that they. always were, and always would be, successful. He had an assured manner as host, and he followed two simple rules which were unique in my experience (fairly wide, despite Willoughby's denigration) of ships' parties. First, he limited the number of his guests to a dozen, which was an unusual beginning, for the average party on board any minor vessel of war in port is more likely to exceed three dozen, all crowded into one small wardroom. Second, by skilful manipulation, he always seemed to have one person speaking at a time; this, too, was an advance upon my previous experiences in which the crowd quickly split into three or four groups, each group making its own babel. These two rules made the parties successful and often memorable, and they were always talked over later. I had noticed these characteristics of the host in earlier parties in Halifax; I now realised that the parties were as well managed as a stage performance. Later, I pointed out to Willoughby that his parties were nothing more than 'Welwyn Garden City discussion circles with ship's gin added to taste', but he was quick to reply, saying, 'They must have better gin in Welwyn than I thought, then.'

The guests were usually fairly well-educated men of action, and their stories were often strange and well-told, for, as Emerson said long ago, Englishmen are far from being the tongue-tied creatures that often appear as Englishmen, in their own legends. We had, on this occasion, the usual unusual range of subjects. Somebody commented upon a small warship's luck in having a magnificent Kurdish rug in its wardroom; Willoughby reacted, delighted by the comment, and began to speak of carpet-dealing in the East; Blake afterwards talked about bargains in gems he had picked up whilst surveying some years before in Queensland; one of the clerks from the legation in Reykjavik had served previously in New Guinea and began to talk about the coral reefs of Australia's North-East coast and the contrast between those southern seas and Iceland; Manston spoke at length and in masterly fashion, on the history of Iceland and its long and erratic association with Britain; this prompted Richmond to talk of Iceland as a stepping-stone for many of the arctic and polar explorers; Blake's friend, the army captain, had been in

Western Greenland on one of the Cambridge University polar expeditions in the mid thirties and contributed anecdotes; then we were all adding our views on the psychology of polar exploration, that most engrossing subject. I think everyone except Warrant Officer Dundass added something to the verbal spate; certainly everyone thoroughly enjoyed himself. Drink went round steadily, but far less swiftly than in normal *conversaziones* of this character. Men drink more slowly when they are engrossed in talking and listening. Nobody got drunk, and departures over the side were as sober as a church outing disembarking from a Thames steamer at Marlow. At midnight the night was as clear as an early English summer evening; I thought of six-metre sails in the Solent or, after a sunny day in a half decker, coming slowly in to anchor in the Hamble River and longed for peace.

We sailed at dawn, picking up our seven cargomen and two sister-escorts, armed trawlers, in the channel.

Thus ended our first trip to Iceland. I was quite certain that I wished to return. Even Willoughby said that he had enjoyed the trip; 'a good deal better than stooging round the remoter meridians of the Atlantic' was his comment. I had a standing invitation to look up Manston on my next trip. Climbing into the ship's boat, he had said that he thought that if I had time he would be able to show me parts of the south-west corner of the island, old boy. I thought that, in the manner of God, I might make time.

꩜

The crew, I learned from underground sources, chiefly Jake, liked Iceland. 'Nice lookers, the women in that town, sir,' said Jake, refusing to essay pronunciation of Reykjavik. 'Some nice blondes. Rather partial to 'em meself. Mitchell got 'old of a very tiddley piece, sir. Went 'ome to dinner twice on watch ashore. Fish and chips and ice cream.' I asked how he liked the town. 'I went out with some of the boys, sir. Dead end. Beer's very weak and not enough women to go round. Still, better than muckin' about in the middle of the ocean, sir. We comin' back, sir?' 'Does Mitchell want to know?' I asked. 'I think he's kind o' interested, sir,' said the steward, ostentatiously sweeping crumbs into his palm.

∿

In the months of so-called warfare in those steeper latitudes we fired no gun in anger, saw no U-boats and only once were spied upon in unseemly manner by a Focke-Wulf 'recce and met man' or, more pedantically, one of the German reconnaissance and meteorological observation planes operating from Norway.

We saw the plane early one afternoon on our second trip north.

'Plane bearing green 175!' yelled one of the bridge lookouts.

I happened to be on the bridge, for, although it was Richmond's trick, the Captain or myself invariably shared watches with the two newcomers in those earlier days.

'Probably Coastal,' said the other lookout.

'Famous last words,' Richmond said, and I was already ringing the alarm bell for action stations, air attack.

The Captain reached the bridge before the gong had stopped. He cursed the aeroplane as he stared through his glasses, and then said succinctly, 'Focke Wulf!'

'You must be hot on aircraft recognition!' I yelled, staring aft to see how the pom-pom crew was closing up, timing them against future accusations of lethargy, although they seemed to be sprinting into action at good speed.

'I am quite good,' replied Willoughby in his sometimes affected Noel Coward manner. 'I have been frequently commended by superior officers!' and then, as an afterthought, 'RN officers!' His glasses still moved with the enemy plane.

The plane was a great distance off, almost at extreme visual range, flying on a north-easterly bearing, as if in a vast semi-circular sweep. The Captain continued his lament: 'Probably on his way home. This'll mean we'll be reported to the local U-boat aces. No sleep tonight, dammit!'

The plane continued to describe its semi-circle; I could imagine the scene in the great plane; the *Luftwaffe* men counting us, merchantmen and escorts, estimating our tonnage (rather more accurate figures, I thought, than Goebbels' propaganda experts would use if we got pipped), probable fire power, course, speed, disposition, and so on. Then suddenly the plane banked, turned to the east and within three minutes was beyond our sight. 'Well, that's over. Not even a shot at the so-and-so,' said Willoughby. 'All right, Number One, we'll keep the gun crews closed up aft. Bunts, grab an Aldis and get some signals cracking!'

The rest of the afternoon was spent in exchanging signals with the other escorts and the commodore of the convoy. Course was altered and zig-zags for the night settled. Finally we all seemed agreed upon procedure and a plan of action if we were attacked. There are always plans available, produced by Admiralty experts for use in such contingencies, but people on the spot will always have ideas of their own which seem to give local colour to the black-and-white sobriety of 'Admiralty Instructions in the Event of, etc, etc.'

We were subdued and fidgety all through the night. At every moment we expected to see the tanker, away on our starboard bow, flame into destruction, or to get a flash from one of the escorts that she had a contact. Willoughby and myself took turn and turn about with the only pair of asdic earphones, listening to the mournful echoes through the seas. Or we walked out from the bridge-house to the bridge. Or drank coffee in deep, grateful gulps. Or leaned over the bridge staring into the pale northern summer night.

And nothing happened.

We steamed on and on and arrived at Reykjavik two days later ...

On the return trip, Richmond told us that three of the men had written home, describing how we had been attacked by 'a giant Jerry aircraft in the middle of the Atlantic'.

'I hope you let them go through.'

'Yes, I thought they were harmless enough.'

'Good, the men must have their fun, and folks at home ought to get something in return for the comforts they knit and the chocolate they go without!'

'The thing that puzzles me,' said Richmond, 'is how they have the face. They know I'm going to read their letters.'

'They probably think you write the same sort of thing,' said Willoughby. 'Don't you?'

Richmond disdained to answer.

Such paragraphs, I commented, had also puzzled me whilst in *Solander*, but I had put the puzzle aside; I had no wish to engage upon 'An Inquiry into the Nature of the Psychology of Sailors'.

'Might be interesting,' said Willoughby. 'You could start with an analysis of your own non-drinking, non-smoking, whoring self. That'd be a puzzle of a sailor for any public!'

I said I considered myself merely an *amateur* sailor.

'That's true enough,' said Willoughby gently, and then with his malicious smile, 'I suppose that's why that ensign aft looks as if it has been decorating a coaling hulk for the last ten years! Get it changed, will you? Don't make it look too professional, of course. Just clean.'

'Aye, aye, sir,' I said.

Willoughby was often unscrupulous with these tactical strokes of his: the ensign was soiled but certainly not grey, but I should have known how touchy the Captain was about such things. As Richmond said on another occasion: 'For a chap who's always running down the RN, the Old Man has a hell of a lot of respect for some of their institutions and ideas.'

The Old Man's three junior officers agreed on that simple fact.

During our second brief sojourn in Iceland I took Manston up on his offer to escort me in the steps of those nineteenth-century British travellers who made a tour to Iceland almost as *de rigueur* as the European tours of the eighteenth century. Unashamedly we made the hackneyed trip to Thingvellir, journeying there with Richmond one Sunday afternoon by bus. The ride was quite as adventurous as any ever made by Ebenezer Mackenzie on the back of an Iceland pony; it was certainly among the more thrilling journeys I have made. The driver apparently thought himself engaged upon an Icelandic bus point-to-point, for he careered along the narrow tracks, which branch off from the main easterly road out of Reykjavik, as if possessed of innumerable demons, a sort of mechanised John Gilpin. A peacetime Donington Park enthusiast would have revelled in the experience. We would see a narrow bridge ahead, spanning a stream of considerable velocity, and beyond the bridge, approaching cars. No matter. To our driver these were occasions for displays of fanatical skill. He accelerated immediately and we hurtled at the tiny bridge like some meteoric missile, missing our opponent by millimetres, crossing the bridge on wings. It was wonderful and incredible, Manston agreed. Richmond was entranced. Even more incredible was the fact that we reached Thingvellir without a scratch on the coachwork.

Thingvellir, a vast national park, is strangely unlike a park to those used to Hyde and St James's, for it is an immense lunar landscape with vistas of lava rifts, canyons, gorges, deserted plains, and always the enclosing background of the distant blue mountains. Manston, continuing as our Baedeker, said that Thingvellir was, indeed, once known as the Blue Woods, but no woods now exist.

Mr Alfred Hitchcock, we decided, could undoubtedly make a truly blood-curdling film with Thingvellir as a background; the park would provide a perfect setting for his studies in the macabre. The resulting film would be banned immediately or break box office records.

There is, however, relief from this sinister desolation. The River Oxara, flooding into the waterfall, and the Thingvallavatn, the largest lake in the island, are beautiful contrasts to the desolate lava fields and harsh landscape, alien and fearful to English eyes. Mile beyond mile of the lava plains stretch out to the hills, with the summit of Skjaldbreider in the distance. A few paths cross the plain, passing beneath great overhanging rocks and cliffs of weird geological structure. All is dead; only the clouds have life.

We went climbing between some of the narrow chasms through which offshoots of the Oxara flow. Beneath us were many deep pools, coloured fantastically in blues and greens with a translucent depth unknown in England. We sat on the edge of a gorge and tossed small Icelandic coins into the pool beneath, watching them disappear, spinning, transmuted and iridescent, into the depths. After losing the equivalent of fourpence halfpenny each in this puerile pastime, we resumed scrambling. Each time we came to a break in the gorge, the vista had changed. The swift changes, from far views of blue mountains to nearer views of the lava fields often overgrown with birch shrub, were breathcatching.

Afterwards we went back to the waterfall where the Oxara plunges into the valley in a great cascade. From the waterfall we tramped back to the small collection of buildings at the coach terminus. There we had tea, gazing out over the Hitchcock setting: a church, a manse, a few outbuildings, and beyond those the desolate plain.

Glancing at the trio in the mirror I thought English naval officers seemed odd visitors to this lunar landscape, but not more incongrous, I felt, than the sightseeing Icelanders in their ill-cut European clothes. Only gigantic beings of Viking mien and dressed in skins of wild and excessively woolly animals would have fitted easily into this sombre setting.

Over tea Manston became educational. Thingvellir, he said, had sacred historical associations for Icelanders, for the Althing, the national parliament, met here, in the open air, every summer from early in the tenth century until the end of the eighteenth. In the latter part of that long span these summer sessions must have presented magnificent spectacles, the plain a great tented encampment, interspersed with booths of turf and stone for the political giants. Earlier, he continued, some of the livelier chieftains were inclined to cut up rough and run amok, to the general discomfiture of the more genial chieftains and onlookers. We were reassured, but slightly saddened, to hear that contemporary Icelanders are more pacific, having already fallen into the democratic habit of discussing things calmly. Richmond wagered our mentor that there was an Icelandic political idiom for our own democratic phrases; for instance, 'Ironing out little differences of opinion', but Manston would not plunge, claiming that his knowledge of the language was academic and not politically colloquial. Upon this note we returned to our demon driver.

In the bus, whilst vigorously brushing down my muddied naval slacks, I was once more made aware of what always seemed to me the least endearing of Icelanders' characteristics.

(I write 'Icelanders' although I can only speak with authority for the inhabitants of Reykjavik.) More in sorrow than in anger, then, I report, in the manner of the returned Victorian Traveller, upon the unconcerned manner in which these people clear their throats in public. Whilst eating in restaurants or travelling in buses one suddenly has these curdling, viscous noises made at one's side. Nobody seems to mind. Manston hissed, above the rattling of the bus, that he had become used to it, but that the custom had rather shaken him during his early days in the island. He added that many of the women were addicted to the habit. I nodded my head gloomily, having already wilted under this observation. Manston's theory was that the habit was probably due to the amount of lava dust in the air, but apart from the scientific or medical reasons it was a disturbing factor in human relationships. He had often been seated next to a family party at dinner; an interlude of throat-clearing occurred, and everybody continued with the meal as if Uncle George had merely said that the mutton was pretty good. Even a series of honest-to-goodness teutonic belches would come as a very welcome arpeggio after this, he said.

I was more sorrowful, noting this custom, because it is not the sort of thing a somewhat romantically inclined traveller expects, and the girls were pretty. Despite Willoughby's mournful prophecies they were also well dressed by European standards, and their fashions obviously derived in a direct line from Hollywood influences. Many of the island's redheads and blondes would have taken high place in any beauty contest. All the girls seemed to be able to speak halting English, usually with a pleasing accent. Manston said that marriage and giving in marriage between British soldiers and the natives was increasing, but that the romances were not exactly blessed by the brass hats. Richmond pointed out that it would be a good idea to encourage the practice if the war were to continue in the Thirty Years' tradition, for the

Icelanders seemed to be even more insular than the British, and anything to rid the world of that characteristic ought to be considered a useful step in human progress.

The Icelandic men were not so prepossessing as the girls. I had expected to find them worthy descendants from ancient viking forebears, upstanding blonde beasts, rather like Norwegians; instead they were pallid creatures, often jaundiced in appearance, and many were hollow-chested and weakly. On the other hand, as Manston pointed out, that same description might be applied by a dispassionate observer, say a Red Indian, to the majority of British tommies, yet we all knew that these gentlemen in battledress could, if necessary, go on for intolerable stretches with most unweakly doggedness.

Yet the Icelandic males seemed to be lacking in any sort of physical vitality or ebullience, and nobody could say that of any group of British soldiers. Occasionally, usually down by the harbour, one saw a well-set-up Icelander, but not often. The fishing fleet was laid up at that time (one or two of the trawlers had been damaged by shellfire from U-boats and the fishermen had declined to sail), and this fact spread depression amongst the men. Perhaps this, and the fact that their country was occupied by foreigners, were the reasons why these gentlemen appeared so passive and lethargic, but Manston said no, they had been that way for years.

The relationship between the luckier members of the British army and the more adventurous Icelandic females was established, it appeared, on an understood and accepted basis of secrecy, but most of the men were denied the solace of feminine companionship: their overwhelming numbers made that inevitable, but others were accepted into family circles and, said Manston, several mammas seemed well-disposed towards the prospect of British sons-in-law.

There is so much daylight and so little night during the short Icelandic summer that we found it almost impossible to get to bed. During our third visit to the island, whilst we were lying alongside waiting for examination of one of the propellers by a technician from the base, I became a confirmed insomniac. I would turn in, take one final glance through the port and seeing the cuprous hills and clouds still touched with sun, would think, 'Soon I shall leave this island and be interminably at sea once more. Maybe I shall never return. I must see all I can see now,' and I arose again and went ashore. I have always been like this in strange and other lands, desperate to crowd my mind with memories against long days and nights ahead, uneasily conscious, too, that life begins to move more swiftly after one's thirtieth year. At thirty, I had recently decided, one is most keenly aware of the value of the present tense.

So I went ashore, wandering, watching.

One evening I came to a crowd round a tricycle salesman. He was selling sweet cakes and hot dogs. I bought a hot dog crushed into a roll with much French mustard, and began to talk to an RAF squadron-leader who was also eating with gusto. He said he was waiting for a ship to take him to Canada: he had already been in the island for three weeks and liked the land and the islanders, but now he wished to be away. He was going out to train the Empire's fledglings, he said, and wanted to get on with the job.

'What sort of meat is this hot dog?' I asked in a pause.

He said 'Pony' and I felt momentary revulsion; all preconceived gastronomic theories were shattered, but I continued to eat. The flesh was rather sweet and pleasant, and on the principle that a pilot who crashes ought immediately to go up again, I had another. The airman said he'd had the same feelings upon learning the truth after his first bite of pony-flesh; he added that introducing the unsuspecting to pony meat was a popular joke by the British on the British in

Iceland, and was thought to be quite funny. (I told Willoughby at breakfast. He thought the anecdote funny and said it might go into the log under the heading of 'First Lieutenant's Hot Pony Orgy'.)

These 'hot pony' stands (as the Captain, on his only nocturnal turn ashore, suggested they should be called) were an institution on summer nights in Reykjavik. Icelanders, often in their cups, hung around the tricycles. Perhaps atavistic memories of their historic past rose within them at such moments, for they occasionally became aggressive, invariably making a set at some of the Norwegian airmen. Maybe the sight of their Scandinavian cousins in uniform infuriated them, but they were unfair contests, for the Norwegians were a husky crowd, and the bouts were brief. The local police, too, were swiftly on the scene. Willoughby contended that the bobbies did their rescue work so efficiently in order to preserve the proprieties, for were the Norwegians not big enough to take on Joe Louis himself? We turned and walked back to the ship: the harbour in those early hours of summer mornings was calmed, and the thin light gave gentle beauty to the sharp silhouettes of the enclosing hills.

'This is one way of engaging in the Battle of the Atlantic,' said Willoughby. 'Personally I prefer it to those convoy occasions which the newspapers call thrilling battles with U-boat packs, but maybe I'm middle-aged.' If this was middle-age, I added, I was senile.

~&

Manston came on board to say he had arranged a visit for that evening to a real Icelandic poet: would I care to come? Willoughby, I knew, had arranged a party and I said yes, most willingly.

'He's a bookseller, too, and you can have a good browse round his shelves.'

We went up past the grey-green cathedral, a most splendid landmark from the sea, but architecturally not so interesting as the Lutheran church in the square; also past the hospital, a most impressive building, as aseptic and simple in design as contemporary Finnish sanatoria.

The poet lived in a small, comfortable, unpretentious house on the outskirts of the town. We were shown into his study by his young, blonde daughter who curtsied and disappeared. He was about fifty; a gentle, abstracted man, seeming more like a professor than a poet. We talked of London, Iceland, journalism, literature. His study was closely packed with books, the major Oxford Dictionary and many subsidiary dictionaries, Fowler's *Modern English Usage*, Partridge's *Dictionary of Slang*. Many novelists from Sterne to Bennett, Trollope to Hemingway crowded the shelves. I was thankful to Manston to be here; in this small room, sipping tea, far from the life of the port, the confines of the ship, the smoke-filled wardroom, the prospect of movement.

The poet was translating Thomas Hardy's *Tess* for the Icelandic reading public: he had translated much of Hardy's poetry. 'A labour of love,' he said, smiling, and explained that the total population of Iceland would be scorned as a market by a London publisher. He talked of English authors, asking for opinions. Then he moved to politics. He was a leading Anglophile in the island, and had written much on the possibilities of Anglo-Icelandic co-operation.

These views had antagonised some of the younger, more aggressive islanders, bitten by the Nazi bug in the early days of the war. The windows of his bookshop had been smashed, but he had seen, in some degree, his hopes partly realised, although sadly enough, he said, as a result of war and not of peace. He was perturbed lest any collaboration which might be established between the two countries during the war might languish in a period of post-war reorientation. The economic adjustments would be immense. 'Your fishermen will not wish you to have fish from Iceland,' he said, 'and there is so little else that we can sell.'

I left with the gift of a signed monograph on Iceland, containing an introduction by the poet. Returning to the ship Manston said that the poet had two sons: one in the RAF, the other a deckhand in a British trawler. 'A practical demonstration of beliefs.'

∽❧

The Borg Hotel in Reykjavik was the local Ritz, and with its lounges, dining-rooms and dance-floor was an entertaining place for a rare evening's fling. Within the Borg the Icelandic commercial nabobs and their women folk dined with British army, naval and flying officers, officers from the merchant fleets of a dozen nations, Norwegian airmen, British and American diplomats, business men, technicians. After heavy weather or severe attacks upon convoys the supply of spirits, particularly whiskey, became low and there was much lamentation in the Borg, but at other times the flow of drinks was unabated throughout the evening. The dining-room which abutted the dance-floor was more crowded than any similar room I had seen during the war. Tables were jammed side by side, and the diners and dancers were crammed as closely together as rush-hour strap-hangers on the Piccadilly line. I went only once, with Willoughby, Richmond and Benson. Dundass had found an erstwhile shipmate in a County class cruiser that was anchored farther north in Hvalfjord and had taken a jeep driver over on a visit to the wardroom of this superior man-o'-war. Perhaps he was wise in what we termed his 'treachery'; in the Borg we sat wedged against a table and a pillar, eating with one hand, for to employ two would have been both dangerous and unfair to our neighbours.

The dance band was conducted by an Englishman who was already legendary. One legend told that he had left England to escape the call-up, another that he had once had an orchestra in Cambridge, another that he was the disinherited son of a clergyman, another that he had fallen desperately in love with an Icelandic maiden visiting London and had pursued her vainly to the north. 'Whatever the truth he's made quite a decent band out of the locals,' said the Captain, with the air of an expert.

'Don't you think, sir, his repertory's a bit limited?' asked Benson.

'Repetitive, certainly,' admitted the Captain.

Such high-flown criticism of the higher arts was an established custom in the ship. To this critical sum I added my observation that the conductor was very slickly turned out.

'He's sure to end his days in Hollywood,' said the Captain, sadly. 'Probably play on an ice floe with Sonja Henie dashing about on skates. Quite a film. Think there'd be anything in a scenario along those lines, Alphabet?'

'It has promise, sir.'

'Don't be pontifical. Go and ask that blonde to dance.'

'Is that a command, sir?'

'Of course it is.'

Alphabet fought his way between diners, tables and the wreckage of many meals. He bowed with suave assurance to the blonde and her escort, smiling orientally upon them both, and led the girl to the floor 'as if he had been a gigolo or head waiter all his life,' said Willoughby malevolently.

'I think you're envious,' I said.

'I'm sure I am. It's a trick I've always wanted to have and never learned. Not even after a thousand nights watching French types at work in Syria.'

The room was full, yet pairs and parties continued to arrive. Tobacco smoke hovered in thick layers from tables to ceiling. Glasses were upset, tumbled and shattered to the floor. Waiters struggled between tables, their brows creased with their tasks of memory, their hands filled with food and drink. The dance band played through its slight repertory again and again. A legation party adjoining our own, with Manston a busy interpreter, ate and drank plentifully for understanding between British diplomacy and Icelandic commerce. Alphabet jigged his way past the table, his arm firmly containing 'a very nice piece' as the Captain admitted. She smiled to her glowering partner: over her pale shoulders and paler *voile* Alphabet gave his Commanding Officer a long, slow wink.

'Two more years,' I overheard an Iceland business man say to Manston, 'and this country will be 100 per cent pro-British.'

'No nation is 100 per cent pro-British,' said Willoughby to me, 'not even Britain, thank God. I think I'll borrow that blonde from Alphabet for the next dance. That chap of hers is about 100 per cent anti-British. Still, here goes,' and he arose to try to pluck his long legs from the welter of chairs, tables, people.

~&~

Manston came on board early the following morning, to ask after our health and to inquire whether Willoughby or myself would care to go on a Coastal Command patrol in a Sunderland. The Captain's reply was definite. 'No thanks, I hate flying as much as I hate cold weather. You go, Number One.'

I went. 'It's really a bit of luck,' said Manston. 'It's quite a new idea on the part of the local RAF and RN chiefs. Supposed to show each other the troubles of the other's job.'

136

A dark, heavy-featured flight-lieutenant in blue battle-dress with a DFC ribbon met me on the timbered landing-stage. We went down into the launch: the engines reversed in a flurry of foam and the craft swung round in a white curve.

Two Sunderlands lay out in the fiord: such squat, comfortable-looking planes, holding an impression of vast, conserved power and a reassuring sense of solidity within their snub noses and big pigeon bellies (would a pilot approve of such a description?). The launch swung in and an aircraftman passed over baggage and kit.

A tall, fair, very young pilot officer was supervising the stowing of some gear. He was curt, rather on his dignity, but soon thawed. I went through from the fo'c'sle into the main cabin. How different the world looks through the window of a plane or the scuttle of a ship! Landscapes become clarified and miniatured, evocative of those precise aquatints and lithographs seen in nineteenth-century guide books. The long line of the coast, 'the nice spot of cirrus' (as the flight-lieutenant termed the cloud formations), and the small tramps and larger tankers lying at anchor alongside, seemed drawn so much more exactly and minutely than life-size. I was reminded once more of my early sailing days off the South Coast when I had always the habit to turn from the stern of the pleasure craft in which I first sailed offshore to regard the Regency terraces and crescents of the town in which I lived; and always the sober facades appeared as if through a reducing glass.

Now, in the Sunderland, I turned from this prospect of the oiling jetties to enter the galley and from there stepped into the stern or tail or fin or whatever the after region of a flying boat is called. The curved, dulled-metal sections of the plane swept aft, away from the eyes in rigid mathematical perfection, as pleasing as the ribs of an ocean racer giving inward form to outward beauty.

Then we were shipshape and ready to go. 'Come up on to the bridge!' called the flight-lieutenant.

We moved round into the wind. The shore began to race past, the ships at the quays receding at a great pace. The engines died for a moment. Then we were off again. Again the roar stilled. Then again, and this time off. Foam splashed and flashed against the windows. Suddenly there was a world-bursting roar as the engines took to the full their tremendous power and we moved into flight.

We lifted. How slowly a plane seems to lift. I wonder whether a Spitfire seems to leave the earth so slowly in the first few seconds of its climb. Now we moved across the world, not very high. Two ships under steam in the fiord seemed scarcely a few feet beneath us, yet they were already models. We began to cross the rutted lunar landscape of the island; volcanic desert and waste; here and there the touch of colour of a solitary farm and huts. Then we were above the sea and beyond, for more than two thousand miles, was 'the steep Atlantick stream'.

I asked whether they had a set programme.

'Normally we've a pretty shrewd idea of what we're supposed to do and which of our own convoys we may see, but we have a pretty free hand if we see anything suspicious.'

I was introduced to the navigator, a young red-headed north-country sergeant, obviously living in his job. I told him I was a navigating officer; after that everything was straightforward, and I got my first lesson in aerial navigation, whether I wanted it or not. For the next hour I was back at school. After the lesson I met the third pilot, a sandy-haired little Scot with a fierce red guardee moustache. He was in the starboard seat: the flight-lieutenant, the captain of the craft, had the port side. After a while I was allowed to take over the starboard pew; this gesture seemed to me an honour of a very high order and I was deeply appreciative of this touching exchange of inter-Service compliments.

We searched and swept over our appointed area, a vast segment of the ocean. The low roar of the engines and the unending ocean gave monotony to the ears and the eyes. This seemed a trial more continuous, less eventful than our own, but perhaps their sudden emergencies were even more lively than our own; but 'lunch is served' broke my reverie and I went down to the galley. The starboard gunner aided by the flying-officer had cooked the meal, a Lancashire hot-pot, which would have got an alpha plus in Manchester itself, then fruit salad and cream, then cheese, biscuits, coffee.

I slept for about an hour after lunch; awoke cold, cramped, and went up on the bridge again. The crew were quiet about their tasks.

'Seen anything?' I asked.

'Not a thing. Sea. Sea. Sea,' said the Captain.

We were out for seven hours, cruised more than a thousand miles, saw no ship, no sign of life. From such a cruise one learned more of the true immensity of the ocean than one could ever gain from a week spent on the bridge of a corvette.

Conflicting impressions remained to fill one's mind. It was reassuring to see how vast an area a U-boat must cover to meet a convoy, how difficult to pinpoint thirty merchantmen in the innumerable miles of this green waste, but it was disturbing to see how very far one might have to sail or row in that small whaler of *Tobias* if we should be unlucky, yet more disturbing to consider the prospects of a Carley float let loose to drift upon the seas below.

We parted with cheery farewells. 'Sorry we didn't meet up with any Huns,' said the Captain. 'They don't often oblige.'

'Shoot up any Nazis, Number One?' asked Willoughby at dinner. 'Or does that only happen to Errol Flynn on the movies?'

The following evening we moved out into the fiord and in the dawn we sailed with three merchantmen of medium tonnage, one tanker and one other corvette. Willoughby was senior escort officer and in the wardroom, over breakfast, the Captain's three junior officers decided that he was rather enjoying himself. Dundass was busy below and couldn't give his opinion. I went out on deck. I had a feeling we should not return to Iceland. I was glad to be away again, but I was beginning to feel about Iceland the way I felt about Northern Ireland – that it was a pleasant landfall – but wished we could get more time ashore so that I might journey inland by truck or pony as far perhaps as Hekla, but, as the Captain said half an hour later on the bridge, I seemed to get around quite a lot for a supposedly seagoing sailor, 'calling on poets, nights at the Borg and jaunts in Sunderlands. Must be rather dreary returning to a corvette. Perhaps that's why the log is twenty-four hours out of date.' I knew I was home, but I could afford to smile. The memories were mine.

Chapter 6
To the South

The convoy was slow, and how slow six knots can be! Down through the Bay of Biscay most tediously, and although I try always to cast my mind back into history when I come to seas not hitherto encountered, I found the buffeting of the Bay no urge to historical reflection, and agreed instead with those many mariners before who have cursed the Bay with its maleficent seas; evocations of Nelson and St Vincent were stilled in the thought that the ocean rebelled against the bounds thrust upon it by the French and Spanish coastlines, and in rebellion turned against all navigators attempting rhumb lines across its span. So, at least, it seemed to us as the Bay affirmed its mood and cast us, queasy and lacklustre, across the bridge.

'Sometimes I like the Bay,' said Willoughby, 'because I know I'm on my way back home, for that is how I see the Med. At other times, I must admit, I think the Bay's a bitch.'

'Is this another time?' I asked.

He jerked a nod as he clutched the rail and tried once more to note the position of the nearest merchantman as she rose high above the convoy upon deceptive crests and then was hurtled into troughs more deep than Bunyan's slough.

~&

Twenty-four hours later we were across the Bay and as if to emphasise that we were well away from its inner tricks and tantrums the Bay was almost calm, but deliverance from nature only placed us more suitably for the unnatural Hun, for the convoy was attacked by two long-range bombers.

From our viewpoint on the starboard, seaward station it seemed but a desultory attack, countered by the heavy ack-ack fire from a pre-last-war destroyer, two corvettes and a trawler on the port stations of the convoy. We were not called upon to fire any guns in anger, for we were at least two miles from the fracas. We merely watched.

The warships and four merchantmen patterned the sky with a spectacular and complicated criss-cross of tracer from their light ack-ack. From the heavier guns of the destroyer dirty puffs of explosions hung like odd scraps of boiler-room waste against the paler clouds: waterspouts rose as bombs fell and missed. The noise across the convoy was not unduly shattering. I watched from the bridge with the Captain. He doubted whether the engine-room staff would have imagined action had the alarm not warned them, although, and he smiled, they would probably be mildly perturbed to hear through the ship's side, the noise and feel of distant explosions as bombs hit the sea. It was exciting, and perhaps unjustifiably satisfying, to look down upon the crew closed up about their weapons. The prospect of action came like a tonic after the boredom of the days out from home, and

Willoughby confided that he had the hope that they might get a chance to show their worth and marksmanship. Instead, we all watched an indeterminate action fought out beyond our range, as if through the wrong end of a telescope. 'Peculiar, this bandstand view,' said Willoughby. 'Curious to think that over there those chaps are trying to knock hell out of each other, and, although we're part of it, we just watch.'

It was an unsatisfactory role, maddening in the detachment which was forced upon us as spectators. It was like watching a fierce, exciting competition, with all one's talents and senses keyed for contest, and then, at the moment of entry into the fray, to have impotence thrust into one's bones. I noticed my hands gripping and ungripping upon the bridge rail, but persuaded myself that this was exasperation and not nerves.

The planes flew off. We proceeded without further interruptions.

1604. *Abortive attack by enemy aircraft*, I recorded in the log, and, later, 1616. *Enemy driven off.*

That was our South Atlantic battle!

❦

I had never visited 'The Rock', as perhaps I now should write with the casual ease of acquaintance, and found excitement in the prospect of this historic landmark. If we should get ashore I would account myself lucky, but wagered dismally with Richmond that we should be kept to our ship and see no sights, and dismally we watched our small convoy take its anchorages upon flashed signals from the base. Some of the ships were Malta-bound, said Willoughby, but there were probably others here we should escort to Freetown. Meanwhile we should wait the pleasure of the Base.

'Have you been here before, Number One?' asked Willoughby, and, on my negative, continued, 'You must try to get ashore if we've half a chance. We could fix it that you take the others. I've seen it often enough. The others can draw lots.'

A pinnace ran out from the shore and a RNVR paymaster-lieutenant came quickly aboard and spoke to Willoughby. I heard Willoughby say 'Good', and return a salute.

'You'll get your wish, Number One. It's now just on fifteen hundred hours. We could give each watch three hours ashore. Get them shipshape. I believe the old boy here is fairly strict on rig of the day.'

The prospect of an hour ashore comes to a ship like a breeze after stifling heat; even the thought of placing shoes upon bare stones of jetties. The watch ashore was swiftly ready for the liberty boat. I went with Richmond. He wanted a new pair of half-Wellingtons. 'Wouldn't shoes do?' I asked, for he could then get them out of the base 'slops', but he scoffed, saying they were not 'dressy' enough, and, more practically, that with half-Wellingtons he did not require to be so mindful of the state of his socks. We walked up through those many flights of 'Jacob's ladder' which lead to the main part of the town. I regarded the architecture with delighted eyes. I had never been so far south in pre-war wanderings and the dirty fawns and cream-coloured houses, with their simple Iberian motifs, had much to hold attention.

We found, against belief, footwear for Richmond, and then went shopping. Bananas, oranges, lemons, dates and figs, loaded us down; even the new half-Wellingtons were filled with oranges. 'We ought not to forget the old man,' Richmond said, and inevitably began to discuss him, asking, didn't I think Willoughby a rum bird?

'Perhaps more interesting than rum,' I said.

'He's rum!' reasserted Richmond. 'He's so cold-blooded. He's generous and just, never loses his temper, but you feel all the time that he's got iced blood running through his veins.

I think he'd do anything or anyone if he decided on a certain course.'

'Is that such a rare quality these days?'

'I think it is a rare quality the way Willoughby has it. He's as detached as a statue about things. He's so damned efficient, too. If I make a gaffe he never bawls me out, just ticks me off in that refrigerator sort of way and then forgets – no, not even forgets – obliterates the whole thing.'

'Isn't that better than bawling you out?'

'It might be with some people, but not for me. I prefer someone who has flaws and foibles. He's too much like a machine that doesn't go wrong.'

I knew too well the quality which baffled Richmond: truly detached creatures are rare in this world, and Willoughby was certainly more detached than any man I had met.

'Wonder what he's like with women,' said Richmond suddenly. 'He's an attractive-looking devil. I imagine he's broken a few hearts in his time. Drives 'em mad I suppose,' but deeming the subject perilously personal, I thought it wise to stay discussion of the Captain's character at that, particularly having well-defined theories of my own upon the subject, and remarked instead that I'd little enough chance to see this aspect of Willoughby's character. Richmond took the hint and we tacitly agreed to discuss the local domestic architecture as we walked round the narrow streets of the rockside town. The streets were crowded with matelots. I noted British, Free French, Norwegian and Polish hatbands. The British sailors seemed gayer than any others, and I wondered again how the legend of the solemn English had originated and persisted. We went slowly. down through the town, across the small footpath by the side of the Rock's tiny hockey ground and stood for a while watching a murderous game between a crew from a battleship and a crew from the Base engineering staff. The Base seemed to be winning. 'Giving 'em a real pasting,' said a Royal Marine, to his mate. 'Not often that old tub's 'ad such an 'ammering. Good job no Eyeties are lookin' on,' but his friend remained unimpressed: 'What else d'you expect? These base wallahs got nothin' else ter do but sit on their arse all mornin' and play 'ockey all the arternoon."

'Presumably from the battle wagon herself,' said Richmond, overhearing their laments.

The afternoon was brilliantly sunny. In the harbour were destroyers, cruisers, and perhaps twenty merchantmen. Aeroplanes zoomed continuously overhead from the Gibraltar aerodrome. No movement of war stirred abroad. At one of the war's pivotal points nothing more martial used the hour than a game of Gib hockey.

We walked slowly down to the liberty boat at our appointed hour.

'Like to come ashore again, Number One?' asked the Captain after I got back on board.

'Oughtn't one of us to be on board?' I queried.

'Not a bit of it. Come on.'

We went, with Benson, who proposed to try to track down a RNVR friend who had a base job somewhere in the town.

'Looks after some local secretarial staff, I believe. Might be some feminine perks about.'

'You'll have to look very lively with your perks, then, Alphabet,' said the Captain. 'Liberty boat's at nine.'

'I'll be there, sir,' said Benson, saluting in the best Dartmouth manner and marching off along the quay.

'It's a sound idea leaving Richmond or Alphabet alone on board occasionally,' said Willoughby. 'Gives 'em a sense of responsibility. In my second week in my first ship I had to move berth in harbour up in Scotland. The Captain and Jimmy were ashore. I did it – with the coxswain, of course, but the whole job gave me more confidence in ten minutes than I'd have gained in ten weeks with the Captain on board.

If anything desperate crops up, they'll cope, and if it's too desperate they'll just have to track me down. They'll try "The Rock" anyway.'

We walked up to the Rock Hotel. The afternoon, with this unexpected extra break of freedom, was wholly pleasurable, and Willoughby's companionship was always enjoyable. He was an amusing talker, possessed of vitality and novelty in his approach to almost any discussion. We disagreed profoundly upon main issues, but our disagreements were so jocular and so lively that our mutual humour was enhanced by discord. Always we agreed in that main issue of our lives, the running of *Tobias*; on that potentially controversial subject our thoughts dovetailed completely. We might not always agree in the first soundings of our views, but gradually we came to agreement in as close an approach to objectivity as two opinionated men are ever likely to get. Occasionally the incongruity of this situation made me smile, for although we might agree to disagree for ever upon some momentous question of ideas (the nationalisation of the land, the inevitability of war, the nature of evil, etc, etc, etc) the beamy hull of *Tobias* could impress us most swiftly into a matrix of uniformity. I once mentioned the incongruity to Willoughby. 'Yes, but *Tobias* is a fact and war is an idea,' he countered, but he smiled even as he voiced his sophistry, and before the comment that a man would be bold to engage in these Hegelian dialectics in this year of grace.

'We shall disagree again, then, if we make *Tobias* into an idea, that is certain,' said Willoughby, 'although it would be interesting to continue our argument, for we might make both war and *Tobias* disappear and I could return to my beloved Levant. Yet if we return and find the four-inch gun uncleaned we shall both agree that it must be cleaned and its lackadaisical crew punished.'

147

I nodded, knowing well that the gun crew of *Tobias* would never find themselves in such a situation, that our four-inch gun was as well kept as any in His Majesty's Navy, knowing, too, that in this belief and in confidence in 'Guns' we both agreed.

That afternoon, climbing the many steps to the hotel, I remember that we continued to talk of *Tobias* and her crew, our discussion arising from Willoughby's contention that a truly civilised and educated man must travel. From this we began to talk of the travels of *Tobias*.

'She seems to be seeing the world,' I said. 'Halifax, Ireland, Iceland, Scotland, now Gibraltar and soon Sierra Leone.'

'If that could be called travel and not merely travail,' said Willoughby, craving permission for his pun. 'The travail is all right in its way, but as a result we are becoming a training ship, like those sailing ships the Scandinavians sailed before the war, or like that ship that Alan Villiers sailed. We shall train our seamen too well in *Tobias* and then we shall lose them.'

'How?' I asked.

'There are two more CW applications – Aston and Mason – which, with Pitchford, make three of our crew anxious to leave.'

CW or Commission and Warrant applicants were those of the crew who wished to present themselves for examination as prospective officers. The applications had come through me, as First Lieutenant, to the Captain. The three men were HOs – Hostilities Only – ratings, all well-educated, Aston from Rugby, the others from grammar schools. I mentioned that it was strange that none of our Petty Officers seemed anxious to apply for a commission.

'I wonder whether it is really odd,' Willoughby mused, 'I suppose the reasons are mainly social.'

I had pondered the problem myself. Perhaps it is the same in the Army and RAF. The practical men rose rapidly, or fairly rapidly, to become Petty Officers or Chief Petty Officers or Warrant Officers. In such positions they had a certain, and often a considerable authority and a respected and defined status on board, but they were not removed in this status from their normal social background. In such positions they rendered invaluable services, services more rare, difficult and technical than most of those carried out by any junior officers, yet having advanced so far, they seemed disinterested in further progress.

'I think mainly the King's English,' I said, for this had long seemed to me the barrier. 'They advance to Chief Petty Officer. They are comfortable. To take a commission means a temporary drop in pay, but more disturbing, a move into a social world in which their accents are often noticeable. They would be uncomfortable and awkward. Life would lose its zest.'

'Would anyone worry?' asked Willoughby.

'Nobody else would; the applicant might.'

'You think the main snag, then, is the wrong accent.' I thought my theories were borne out by the overwhelming ratio of ratings to Petty Officers as CW applicants, a higher ratio than actually existed in the Service.

'Perhaps you are right,' said the Captain. 'It would be interesting to have official figures. Perhaps we ought to start an elocution class in the dog watches. That should be a job that Alphabet would like.'

I was quite certain that Benson would like the task; it would suit his histrionic gifts, but equally certain that my own responsibilities would noticeably increase if the crew's working hours were to be complicated by meditations upon English vowel sounds, and the thought that the helmsman might wish to pass his time declaiming in refaned and flutelike tones that the rain in Spain lies mainly in the plains, was too gruesome a prospect. From our conversation whilst ascending the acute paths of the Rock, no bold and profound sociological experiments in one of HM ships were dated.

Two hours later we returned to find that no crisis had developed. *Tobias* swung at her anchorage as discreetly as any warship that ever hunted a U-boat.

⤴

'To Freetown, then,' said Willoughby the next morning at breakfast. 'That ought to be a thrilling destination for all officers in *Tobias*. Anyone been there before?'

Benson had, once. His destroyer had made a trip there early in the war.

'Not exactly Hollywood's idea of the tropics,' he said. 'I found no Lamour there, and damn little glamour, but quite interesting as an experience. Once!'

⤴

'This bleedin' Freetown run is getting me down,' said one of the crew three days later, and, overhearing him, I silently agreed. I climbed to the bridge, smiling as I heard him elaborating his dirge. 'Nothing but n******, I suppose, and sweat. Why in the name o' Christ does the British Empire 'ave to go in for grabbing these God-forsaken places right off the map.' Somebody said it probably wasn't off the map, and the argument quit Freetown and launched into a tricky debate upon Imperialism. That, I knew, would occupy 'blue' watch, now off duty and lazing through their dog watch, until one of the after lookouts called to them, 'What about somebody taking over my watch?' I should hear their stirrings and shufflings, their curses and grunts as they became once more active service seamen, putting aside disputation, climbing to their rightful stations.

The afternoon sun burned steadily, shrivelling the air that sought to cool our bodies and our tempers. From time to time a slight breeze moved past us, but these were wisps, as if some skylarking god (or perhaps goddess) had shaken a celestial handkerchief before our faces, then plucked it from us so that we should once more endure the shimmering heat. Sweat oozed down my back, beneath the white cotton shirt I sometimes wore to give some semblance of official splendour to the bridge. I felt the steady runnels down my spine. 'In a moment this rivulet will reach my coccyx,' I told myself, and this fearsome thought gave me a sort of miserable pleasure, perhaps masochistic, although I preferred to think it was the bizarrerie of the phrase that caused me to smile and not delight in discomfort or in any personal psychical problems.

I had the afternoon watch. The Captain was trying to sleep; Number Two also. Number Three, seated on a stool in the upper wheelhouse, was dealing with a batch of signals and confidential papers. The ship was heavily silent, somnolent under the sun. This silence held the world, so that the throb of the engines, the voices of the crew, even the fall of a spanner upon the deck plates, became merged into a murmur as unheard as the noises of the countryside in a sweltering afternoon, and continuing in reverie I thought of afternoons of my childhood when such murmurous silence lay upon the downland farms my Uncle Taff often visited, silence that brooded over the county, although far away were the whistle of a train, the wooden clack of reapers, the bleat of sheep.

I looked to the convoy again: a destroyer, three corvettes, and five large merchantmen. Station-keeping throughout the convoy seemed to be of a high order, although it would be difficult to indulge any pronounced personal view concerning station-keeping on such a copybook day and I returned once more into my memories, as all sailors must often return.

❧

Five days later we stood off Freetown. 'A bloody funny name for the place,' said one of the ratings who had apparently been there. 'The only things free are sweat and syph!' and he drew his hand across his neck, dripping with sweat.

No sea breeze cooled us; the heat was almost unendurable. A step from the wheelhouse to the bridge was excessive, a wearing demand upon the body. On the bridge we all wore khaki shorts and sandals: that was all. The sun burned our bodies, but worse than the heat was the suffocating air. Even breathing was a conscious effort, and almost painful when we sought to sleep. Clean sheets upon the bunk gave but momentary relief, for within the minute that fresh linen soothed the flesh, the air of the cabin closed in, pressing down upon the body like a heavy, dank, smothering blanket. Any movement in the open air or on the bridge was something to evade. Within the hull of the ship steps were torture. Even the necessity to descend to a cabin or the wardroom offered nothing but unwelcome effort and was delayed. We thought often of the poor devils in the engine-room. For them there was no respite, only the heat and the heat and the engine-room stench of oil and much-used air.

'It's bloody hot, doon there, Number One,' said the Chief Engineer as I met him by the bulwark, our passage already ended. He was mopping his face with an oily handkerchief. 'D'ye ken we get ashore in this doomp?'

'I think so, if you want to. How're they standing up to it down below?'

'They're guid lads. Feel better noo it's ended for awhile. They're very reasonable about things, all things considered. Groose a bit, but who wouldn't? T'would be bonny the noo with a nice wee bit o' fried fish ahead.'

'Well, you'll probably get an orange here.'

'God pity indeed the poor bastards who get landed in shore jobs yon place,' he said.

I pitied them, too, watching the heat upon our plated deck, imagining that sun beating down upon the corrugated iron roofs of the town. Beneath our awnings was shade of sorts, but the sun shafted relentlessly down through gaps in the cloth, cutting through the darkened patterns in burning strips of light, dazzling to the eyes.

'The biggest boom in the world,' said Benson, from the bridge.

'Is that something to be proud of?' asked Richmond, tiredly.

'It is probably their only boast,' as if apologising for the Freetown naval authorities. 'My friend in Gib,' continued Benson, 'was here for a while in one of the depot ships. He told me they had to delouse the bread before eating. Seriously. He is one of the few men in the Service who thought that being posted to Gib was a soft number.'

❧

I went ashore the following day. Why? I ask now. Curiosity could be the only lure, although from the sea Freetown carries no hint of its abounding dreariness.

'You might get some curios or some fresh fruit, Number One,' said the Captain as I descended, after Benson, into the crowded liberty boat. 'These blackouts around the ship handle the stuff too much for me.'

The natives, or 'Mr Blackouts', paddled their tree-trunk canoes alongside the ships' anchorages throughout the day. 'Changey for changey' was their recurring theme, with much pigeon-English profanity besides, and the crew, as experimental as any sailors, brought out their ragged flannels and underpants or their duty-free cigarettes and bargained in barbarous language for bananas, mangoes, pineapples and coconuts.

Once, after listening from the bridge, I recorded an exchange of pleasantries for a letter home. The native, as colourful as a Gauguin painting, self-possessed, ingratiating, his antique craft loaded with fruit, called to the deck lookout his perpetual cry, 'Changey for changey!'

LOOKOUT: Changey for what, you big black bastard?

NATIVE: Changey-for-changey!

LOOKOUT: What do you want for that pineapple? No, that one, there, Rastus. (Aside, to another of the crew) Got any beads? That's what Livingstone always give 'em, wasn't it?

SECOND LOOKOUT: Or bits of old looking-glass. They like looking at theirselves. He probably wants some clothes.

FIRST LOOKOUT: I should think a pair o' shorts wouldn't do 'im any 'arm, the way 'e's sitting there showing all 'e's got. 'Ere Rastus, what about that pineapple?

The bargaining continued. Somebody, trying to sleep on deck, called plaintively for them to 'put a sock in it and *buy* the bloody thing', but the deck watch had two more hours to go and such an interlude made handsome inroads into the afternoon watch. They got their pineapple, after twenty minutes' rude bargaining, for an old 'flannel' (the naval rating's vest with blue border) and four cigarettes.

'That's about eightpence. Talk about profiteering. My old woman could a made a pair o' drawers out o' that flannel.'

'Eat yer bleedin' pineapple, forget yer old woman and 'er drawers and pipe down for Christ Jesus' sake,' cried the voice of the plaintive sleeper.

Somebody went off for a knife, and the heavy slumbrous heat closed once more upon the ship.

⟞✦

The liberty boat ran in to King Tom jetty. The NAAFI canteen was closed until 4.30 a notice decreed. The matelots groaned aloud.

'And there's sure to be no beer in stock,' said a knowledgeable one. Many of the crew joined the jostling queue for the lorry which would take them out to Lumley Beach for a swim.

'I don't think I could rustle up enough energy to swim,' said Benson. 'What happens now? Do we walk?'

It seemed that we did. My second trip ashore was with the Captain and Dundass who, after a long sojourn in the base, knew the ropes and got us all a lift, but that afternoon we trod the sunbaked, circuitous road past the naval barracks towards the town, avoiding the more direct route down to the native village, heavily labelled 'Out of bounds'.

'My friend at Gib,' said Benson, 'often wondered whether that notice was put up to preserve HM Officers and men from the evils of the flesh, or to ensure that they didn't get too keen an insight into the squalor of the native quarters. The stream, I understand, provides washing, bathing and general sanitation facilities for the locals.'

'You're a bolshie, Alphabet,' I said.

'Not really, Number One. I'm a retailer of other people's anecdotes. Always have been.' We scrambled over obstructions of broken boats and driftwood on the beach. The village lay along the sandy foreshore. Villagers stared at us with bland inquiring eyes. Behind them was the huddle of mud, straw and bamboo huts which made their homes. They sat in groups around the entrances, jabbering discordantly.

'No uncultivated native tongue is ever satisfying, tonally,' said Benson, and I remembered his interest in music. 'Curious, that. I've often wondered whether the more civilised natives of the South Seas talk more musically. With luck, I may be able to find out at the Navy's expense.'

We came to the outskirts of the town. There were signs of stone buildings, or rather buildings with evidence of stone beneath patchings of wood and rusted corrugated iron. A foetid stench came from the native fish market; a million flies were also patrons. On the opposite side of the road was a native food market: vividly coloured fruits and a miscellaneous collection of beans seemed the staple diet. Amongst the crowds of natives moved a few local celebrities, opulent enough to possess umbrellas. They moved sedately, pompously, self-important in their incongruity.

The roads, by now, had gained in hygiene. Immense gutters, almost trenches ('dangerous in the dark,' said Benson) were dug alongside the footpath.

'Emporia!' said Benson, waving airily to the ramshackle buildings with their trays of trinkets, raffia baskets, earthenware and coloured leather novelties. A few matelots turned over goods: none seemed keen to buy. Another group stood outside one of the dingy-looking beer bars.

'God help any man who tried the local jungle-juice,' said Benson heartily. 'I should think its effects are swifter and more malignant than those of any other drink ever concocted.'

We came to the town: a new YMCA building, the local hospital, a few shops, another NAAFI canteen and, on the opposite side of the street, another native market and more flies. The sun was insistent and the air heavy, wet, oppressive.

'Shall we go up to the Syrian quarter?' asked Benson.

I thought we might.

The Syrian quarter of Freetown is more substantially constructed than the area we had crossed. Several of the shops contained silks, scents and trinkets in considerable quantities; some seemed almost overstocked with rolls of cloth. Almost every shop seemed to have an antique and well-used sewing machine outside. I wondered how many traders, engaged in similar trades and cut-throat competition, could make a living in these poverty-stricken areas. A few beautiful Syrian children played in the street, as unconcerned as salamanders in the molten heat. Their great dark eyes gazed upon us in unhurried, easy curiosity. 'Not really so poverty-stricken just about here,' said the cynical Alphabet. 'Most of the rest of the town is, though, but the universal soya bean keeps body and soul together and they don't have to have chicken for dinner every night like RNVR types!'

I thought of 'Soya Link', that tinned concoction of soya bean and pork which had already appeared on the wardroom table since leaving Gibraltar. It had not been very heartily received; Jake had been somewhat defensive about its appearance on the menu, promising to see that it should be kept from us in future, if humanly possible.

We bargained for, and bought, some cotton prints. They would do for coupon-restricted friends in London, I thought, and turned to watch the worldly Benson, bargaining harshly for lurid silks: he had commissions for several lengths of cloth, he said, and projected an extra speculation in silk for personal profit.

'Pure smuggling, in fact,' I offered in uncritical but objective comment.

'Not really, you know, Number One. I always like to think that smuggling is for oneself or when one has a buyer waiting, anxious to take stuff off your hands as soon as you dock. After all, I may be forced to keep this stuff. Sheer loss, old boy. I may even be forced to have my civvy shirts made out of the damned stuff.' I smirked, interested to learn that the Captain was not the only sophist on board, avid for the sight of Lieutenant Alphabet Benson, RNVR, in shirts of the palest pink sheer silk.

We wandered back to the railway station, thence to Admiralty Wharf, bought more fruit, and, for once, longed for the liberty boat to take us back to the ship. It would, at least, take us from the soul-tainting town of Freetown.

Later that evening, whilst in the bridge-house, I heard one of the lookouts say to 'Bunts': 'A Blackamoor offered me 'is sister for a shilling this arternoon, Bunts.'

'Did you take her on?'

'No.'

'Why not?'

'Dunno. Didn't fancy the idea. Don't seem right some'ow. Besides it was so bloody 'ot. I like getting 'ot on the job, not before it.'

'Something in that, chum.'

The explanation, I thought, might not have appealed to the late Havelock Ellis, but as an approach to Freetown's frolics the laconic explanation seemed eminently practical, adequate, and commendable to the eavesdropping officer in the bridge-house.

Willoughby held none of his special parties during our three days in Freetown, and only went ashore on the third day to get instructions from the Base. I went ashore with him to see whether Hughes might be about, but his corvette was out on patrol and would not return for at least a week. Meanwhile, we used the days in deckchairs placed beneath the awnings rigged on the boat deck, gazing at the shore, perhaps the only satisfying manner of absorbing Freetown into experience. I had no wish to repeat my trip ashore. Jake made many iced lemon and orange drinks and we drank of these, copiously and perhaps foolishly, but we would soon be away, we knew, and that thought gave us freedom from too great worry, and, anyway, our water was safe enough with its too-evident flavour of chlorination.

We sat and yarned, the occupants of the three deckchairs changing throughout the day. We ranged over an improbable miscellany of subjects, moving from philosophical gambols to simple narratives with ease and no sense of disproportion. I think we all enjoyed these times of chatter.

Willoughby always held the floor (or perhaps 'deck', more correctly) when he spoke, for he seemed much older than any of us, and his views and experiences were always richly and ably expressed. Richmond offered opinions as if he were sceptical of their value as contributions to any subject, but they were always so modestly phrased and so balanced in outlook that we turned to him always with interest, and gradually, although his modesty remained, his confidence increased so that he entered into all arguments, even those upon seamanship and the strategy of sea-warfare, our more expansive subjects. Benson's were worldly contributions: his mimicry and bland self-assurance were entertaining and welcome variations. He had, too, the born actor's sensitive understanding of atmosphere, and if we were too dulled by heat, apathetic and irritable, his tales began more cunningly and he built up the atmosphere he required for livelier tales, and always, at the end, he had us where he wished, laughing immoderately, caught between desire to continue listening and desire that he would leave us to fight the heat without these complications of exertion.

The fifth member of the changing group was frequently the Chief Engineer who was almost always silent. Sometimes Willoughby tried to draw him out, but conversationally Dundass was not to be cosseted. He was self-possessed and less shy than Richmond (or even than myself, I sometimes thought), but he preferred to listen, he said with his pawky Scottish smile. He was in fact, he said, one of the world's foremost listeners in the same way that Lieutenant Benson was one of the world's foremost talkers, and he smiled as Benson, imitating Whistler, took a fencing stance, saying 'Touché, Chief'. Even in the heat, that histrionic gesture, making tremendous inroads into a man's slight store of energy in those low latitudes, was made profitable to Alphabet by our laughter.

The crew also had their conversational moments. One afternoon I overheard a languid exchange of naval lore and reminiscence:

'When I was under training in Plymouth last summer, rig o' the day was piped as number threes, negative Jumpers.'

'Muster bin 'ot.'

'Cos it was 'ot. And I seen a destroyer comin' in at 'Arwich, seven o'clock in the evenin', and all in 'alf whites.'

'Muster bin 'ot.'

'Cos it was 'ot, stoopid.'

'Not as 'ot as now, eh?'

'No, nor so many daft bleedin' matelots about as now.'

'Muster bin nice.'

This judgment was followed by guffaws from the tired, clammy listeners, and then silence.

∾

Sleeping was the most complex of our problems. We would doze during the day, fitfully and unrestfully in the deckchairs, but at night, within the stifling confines of our mosquito nets, sleep evaded us like a vision beyond the power of man to hold. At first we tried to sleep below, with the fans going flat out, but relief was negligible, and we brought mattresses to the boat deck, flung them down and built our nets into low protective huts about us, but the clammy night defied this ruse and we slept unhappily. I remember such uneasy nights as interminably long, and the need for sleep, in a time of much leisure, insistent and unsatisfied.

The crew, being perhaps tougher, having perhaps less leisure, slept rather better than their officers, but amongst them also, insomnia began its tricks, and through the night there were the stirrings of men waking between their brief slumbers to smoke a shielded cigarette, to stare within their nets, at worlds far beyond the Freetown boom, doubtless towards homes and families away in the colder but more restful north.

❧

There was one more leg in our journey to the south, to Lagos. It was Freetown again as far as *Tobias* was concerned. None of us had any great desire to go ashore. I went, as part of a programme of self-discipline, for I had made a rule quite early in my career as an amateur sailor that I should visit and indeed try, to get beyond the outskirts of the port, perhaps to the hinterland, in mild exploration. This I had done in Iceland, with satisfactory answers to curiosity. In temperate climates this curiosity concerning strange lands is a desire felt by all on board, but in those tropical regions the desire went. It was easier and more comfortable to stay on board: the effort of descending a ladder to the liberty boat was overwhelming, sweat soaked our shirts long before we got ashore. Little wonder we kept to deckchairs and our lethargy.

On my first trip ashore in Lagos, however, I was lucky, making acquaintance with an American executive official of Pan American Airways. Jimmy Marchbanks was pleasant, friendly, hearty. He had a great interest in the local people, their customs and habits, and had made many notes, he said, concerning these aspects of the life surrounding his bungalow. He had, for instance, collected a list of names bestowed upon, and answered to, by the natives, or 'wogs' as everyone seemed determined to call them. The names were remarkable and colourful.

I remember Sylvanusk, Ojo, Amiloa, Moses, Bassie. On the promise of gentle badminton, a cold shower, an open-air movie show and a leisurely breakfast with pineapple juice and waffles I stayed overnight at his Pan-Am quarters.

At night, in company with his staff, we were shown a film with Miss Dietrich as an alluring creature caught into a whirlwind of wild west action. Occasionally during her giddy saloon-bar life a lizard crawled over the screen, moving across her slender, slightly-dressed charms in hideous sloth. The masculine audience groaned, for this seemed no way to treat Miss Dietrich, however two-dimensionally celluloid her charms. The following morning Jimmy's house-boy, Moses, dressed in a yellow robe too long and too brilliant, woke me by tugging at my mosquito net. He smiled broadly as he placed pineapple juice and tea on the small bedside table. Over breakfast, my host yarned about his service. He enjoyed it, he said, but longed for his year of service to be over, and for the five weeks 'rehabilitation course' he would get in the States. 'Another way of saying furlough, I guess. I'll enjoy it just for the chance of knocking off these damned quinine tablets,' and he fingered his 5-grain tablet with hostile eyes.

He spoke of the local harvest festival which had just begun. 'It will go on until the second week in December, almost four months. Quite a festival. The three local religions – pagans, Christians and Muslims – celebrate in different months. Most of the pagans are farmers. They're pretty good at sacrificing sheep and fowls. Kinda bloody. The Christians get going in church. Everybody is blessed on the altar by the pastor. Money pours in. Local money, that is. Probably worth about a dime and a bit back home. A bazaar follows the church service. Gets kinda lively. Then the local courting couples get going. The Muslims carry on in much the same way. They vary the days, of course. It's a pretty swell affair whilst it lasts.'

He talked amusingly about the natives. He had that same interest in the people that I imagine a few of our own soldiers and surveyors develop when based in outlandish spots. He thought his 'assignment' could have proved much worse. 'Especially when I think of some of your poor devils in the desert, or even people like yourself. I do get breaks occasionally. I got a one-day trip into nearby French territory recently. We got permission from the governor of the territory and a beautiful new French franking on our passports. Odd, isn't it, considering the state of France today. Anyway, it was all OK. I liked the French towns. Clean wide streets, palm trees, the old Atlantic. Very picturesque. We traded whiskey, soap and cloth for some real champagne, cognac and perfume. God knows how they keep their stocks up. They seem to be able to do it easily, too. Ran into a French missionary, too. Jeez, but he was a husky, black-bearded guy. We were told he'd been in the Foreign Legion and had done wonders. Croix de Guerre and all that stuff. He seemed a swell fella!'

He talked on. He said he liked talking, and as his anecdotes were enthusiastic and interesting I liked listening, thinking, too, that if Pan-Am made this curious and inquiring type of mind one of the qualifications in overseas employees, they showed unusual foresight.

I have pleasant memories of Jimmy Marchbanks of Pan-Am: his richly monotonous colloquial Manhattan voice, racing on and on with his anecdotes, his splendid hospitality and his cold, cold shower. We exchanged London and New York addresses, promising to look each other up in the piping days of peace, but even as I write these words, I realise that all this took place three years ago, and peace seems still some distance off.

꙳

We came up from the south after one more trip between Gib and Freetown, and then were ordered northwards again, to England, as escort to an uneventful convoy. 'They will not let me stay in the sun,' said the Captain, as we moved across the Bay. 'I'll bet you ten bob, Number One, that they shove us back on that Atlantic racket straightaway!' and he grimaced. The prospect seemed ugly to me, too, but I had reservations concerning Freetown and the sun. 'We may get back,' I condoled, but he was adamant in depression. Benson, who was also on the bridge, had other views: 'Even if there's fog in the Channel, snow in the Irish Sea, sleet in the Clyde and hail in Belfast Lough, I shall be happy,' he said, and then, to the Captain, maliciously, 'How is it, sir, that you like this kind of climate?'

'This kind of climate is not to be compared with the Mediterranean, Benson, but it does have some sun.'

'I see, sir.'

'I doubt that, Benson. I doubt very much whether you even see that the jack is six inches lower than it should be. Perhaps you will mention that fact, with my compliments, to the First Lieutenant and see whether, between you, it may be rectified.'

'I don't really think the Old Man does like this climate, Number One,' said Alphabet later, lolling in my cabin.

'I don't think so either,' said Number One, as he climbed from his bunk for the afternoon trick, and pulled on shorts, rig of the day.

❧

We put into Liverpool, leaving our charges at the entrance to the Mersey, and went ashore to sample briefly the sombre joys of that northern port. The following morning we received our orders. We would proceed to Northern Ireland, presumably to take up once again that dreary routine of the Western Ocean.

First, however, there was the matter of our boiler clean, and this prospect dimmed all visions of the autumn storms which would soon await us. Each watch could have six days' leave, clear of travelling, the Captain said, and the life of the men about the ship moved more swiftly and exuberantly with this imminence of freedom. Their sudden enthusiasm moved Willoughby to near-bitterness. 'Ask these men to see the lifeboats' stores are ready before they put to sea and they'll dodge the job if they possibly can. Ask them to do the job now when they're going on leave, and they'll do it as if they might need the stores tomorrow. God rot their souls! They're nothing but a gang of pressed men.'

I had come to know them perhaps more closely and might not be so harsh in judgment, yet there was truth in his words. Sometimes they infuriated me. They did so much to harm themselves. The Captain's own example was true enough. They thought always of the moment and rebelled against those duties which seemed without immediate purpose. We trained them, or caused them to be trained, mercilessly in many divisions of their lives at sea, particularly in boat drill and in gunnery. Often they resented the hours spent at the falls or in pulling, obeying orders which seemed to fall so harshly upon them. Some stared sullenly upon me as they went below or came aboard after these exercises, and sometimes I thought that one or two might well be disposed to place a jack-knife between my shoulder blades, as if I were monstrous in sadism and wished to torture them in pleasure. Yet now all was forgotten. I could have placed any of them upon a flippant errand, engaged them upon some arduous employment, and they would willingly have used the hours, lost in rosy images of their spells ashore. Yet perhaps we are all like this: the only difference that the images are made in degrees of subtlety or sophistication.

❦

The following morning orders came from the Base that our boiler clean had been postponed, that *Tobias* was needed as escort to a westbound Halifax convoy. No words can measure the depths of our gloom. The men moved sullenly about the ship, their exuberance of the previous day submerged within intolerable hatred of Their Lordships and 'They', a mysterious collective designation for all staff officers who had plotted our leave away and plotted us instead into, and upon, one of their vast wall maps of the Western Ocean. The men were at one with the officers in this depression. We were united against all men who served ashore. We revictualled and refuelled and the following afternoon left again for that overnight anchorage which we habitually held the night before a rendezvous.

Yet our hearts were not gloomy for too long a time. 'They must be very short o' ships to be sending a wheezing old tub like this on an escort job, mustn't they, sir?' asked Jake.

I agreed that they must.

'Praps we're the Flying Dutchman, sir, and won't never see 'ome again.'

'Well, what's the Flying Dutchman got for supper?' asked the Captain, coming into the wardroom. (Perhaps I should mention, in passing, that the Flying Dutchman's officers sat down to chicken and plum pudding.)

'Well, we shouldn't have got this ashore,' said Richmond, always the philosopher, as we morosely devoured our dinner.

'Aye, and we shouldna been sleeping to the roll of this blooody old cow tonight. I shoulda been sleeping with ma old woman in ma own wee bed and I'd 've been happy to dine on cauliflower for the privilege,' said Warrant Officer Dundass, in what was probably the longest and most fluent pronouncement ever made by that officer during all his time in HMS *Tobias*.

Chapter 7
North Sea Interlude

L etter-writing at sea or in port is a craft which brings
rich rewards, and the wise wartime mariner maintains
a wide epistolary acquaintance if he wishes to return from
voyages to find words from friends and some evocation of his
own real world awaiting him. Those who do not persevere
in such courtesies are loud in lamentation when the mail-
bag is brought on board and distribution begins. Willoughby
wrote no letters, claiming that no captain adequate to his
tasks at sea *and in port* (he always emphasised the words 'and
in port') could spare time for such indulgences, but at other
times he confessed that he had no taste for such exercise and
that he could do no more than scribble postcards to relations
or to his 'fleshpot' friends, and mainly postcards he received
in reply. Benson and Richmond wrote long letters and gained
longer letters and heavy parcels in return. The Captain
scowled sardonically at the sight of their trophies upon the

wardroom table. 'Every day like Christmas,' he said more than once, seeing us unpack books, cakes and even utilitarian socks, and when I unwrapped a new Gieves tie from Aunt Ruth he sniffed and mentioned that some officers seemed to think the Navy a fancy dress affair, and would we like to organise a tiddley dance for the local Wrens? but the three junior officers, rich in treasure, were banded together against such barbs and smirked their superiority, and I knotted and sported my tie that same evening in his company ashore. We dined at the Grand Central and I saw him gaze fixedly at the tie, but I would not rise, for once wisdom having come with experience.

I heard occasionally from Hughes, my companion in *Solander*. He had moved down to Lagos and to Freetown and pottered round those desolate parallels with no hope of release for at least another year. He had been unluckier than ourselves with our uneventful trip. His own life was dull, 'unrelieved by women or Wrens' he wrote ungallantly, and he continued into long accounts of sweated labour and the unimaginative outlook of Their Lordships in thus condemning him to 'tropical rig and tropical rot'. I also heard from Dick Ives, that gay, inconsequential creature in whose six-metre I had crewed before the war and who had introduced me to the war at sea. He was now in command of a Motor Torpedo Boat (or more usually MTB) in Coastal Forces, working out of an East Coast port, a logical transition for a peacetime helmsman of such demoniacal purpose. 'I got into this racket by the usual Service mixture of blarney and servility. Someone I knew knew someone who knew someone and here I am. I went back to *KA* to do a course of celestial navigation, a course I should have thought more useful to corvetteers like yourself than to small-boat types like meself. Anyway, a pleasant time was had by all and after serving as "Jimmy" in one of the more antique craft round these waters

I was lucky enough to get my own command. The life isn't quite so lively as newspaper stories might have you believe. We're lucky if we run into trouble once every two months, but we spend quite a number of evenings looking for it. Actually if you could get over here for a day or so I could arrange to take you out on one of our parties. I think I could square the old man here. He's a very pleasant RN commander (dug-out), sometimes bewildered by his charges, but a kind old buffer in his way. Do try and get over from London if you can on your next leave.' He continued for three more scrawled pages to describe his life. He had picked up a 'gong', a Distinguished Service Cross, I gathered, on one of his forays for trouble. He said it was a surprise, but quite a pleasant alternative to the usual notes he received from Their Lordships which were invariably intimations that he had overdrawn his pay. He seemed to have slipped into his true place in the war and I found no difficulty in evoking an image of the bland Lieutenant R S Ives, DSC, RNVR, arranging an East Coast life to his entire satisfaction and probably the satisfaction of his crew.

❧

We did get leave after our next trip to Halifax and back. The outward trip was peaceful, but the return voyage was more eventful: we lost two ships and one U-boat was sunk, but we heard nothing of its destruction and had no part in its pursuit. During our return we had one poignant reminder of the war which continued in Europe and which we were sometimes liable to forget. Far to the north of Rockall, that desolate humped island in the Western Approaches, one of the lookouts called 'Object bearing two hundred green', and instantly the crew were taut and all guns were brought to bear. (How impressive that 'all' appears as I write its three alphabetical characters! yet how slight an armament our one four-inch gun, four Hotchkiss and pom-poms aft appeared as we swung them round, and even one of the Hotchkiss was always blind abaft the wheelhouse!)

'It's a lifeboat,' said Willoughby, his glass grim against his eye. 'Now for a depressing half-hour. Probably all dead. Nobody seems to be moving.'

We moved slowly towards the drifting boat, leaving the convoy well to starboard. Ten minutes later *Tobias* towered above a large lifeboat with the simple legend, ELSA: TRONDHJEM painted simply on the stern. Nobody was in the boat. We looked down into a smashed and tillerless craft, our eyes roaming soberly over the split, fallen mast, rotten canvas, and broken thwarts. The bilge boards were awash.

'Strange,' said Willoughby. 'Wonder what happened. Nobody will ever know, I suppose. Probably some Norwegians who tried to escape and got shot up.'

'What about the bodies?' said Richmond.

'Washed overboard. Easy enough. Strange she hasn't sunk, though. Must've come a thousand miles. She ought to be sunk. Put a burst through her, Number One.'

Norwegian-built lifeboats are difficult to sink with machine-gunfire and after fifty rounds we gave up, for the boat still rose resiliently upon the crests and hung listlessly in the troughs, as if unwilling to leave the wide ocean.

'We'll ram,' said Willoughby. 'She's large enough to be a mild menace to shipping.'

A glancing thrust from the modest tonnage of *Tobias* was sufficient to stove in the side planks of the boat and turning away we left her slipping beamways below the surface, filling, dying. We rejoined the convoy: I suspect that none of us on board could keep his mind from the lifeboat, conjecturing upon its fate, the fate of whoever had made its crew. The episode recurred to my mind for weeks and is seen most clearly in the writing of these words so long after the dismal day.

~&

Although sceptical after our previous disappointment, the imminent necessity or prospect of a boiler-clean still brought hope of leave. Ultimately all depended upon the decision of the engineer in charge of the Base: a Commander (E) RN, old, humourless, crusty. During the first afternoon in, the 'Chief' went up to the Commander's office to report the state of our engine-room. 'We should be having that boiler-clean this time, God knows,' he said furiously, righteous in anger. 'Dammit we've noo done nigh six hundred hours and those bleeding engines want looking at after four hundred and a boiler-clean's imperative at five.' He rolled the 'r' in 'imperative' as imperiously as an emperor; and went in hopefulness and anger, for the time before he had been told he must squeeze one more round trip out of his wheezing boiler-room. Now he would see.

'Good luck with that plumber, Chief,' I said as he went down the ladder to the quayside.

'Aye, and I'll be needin' ye're guid wishes, Number One, if I'm t'deal with the hard-hearted son of a bitch who wouldna give ma ticket last time in,' he said, and he rolled off towards the ancient gutted cruiser that lay alongside the far quay and housed the Base Captain's staff.

He came back in half an hour, his broad red face suffused in cherubic glow.

'Old Dundass looks more like a sunflower than a Chief,' said Willoughby, watching him climb on board. 'Has he throttled that Commander E or has he been downtown?' (Downtown being Willoughby's abbreviation for the more resounding titles of those hotels which were favourite stopping-off places

171

for worldly wise old-timers en route to the pleasures of the town.)

'Sir, we get our boiler-clean,' said the Chief climbing ponderously to the bridge.

'Good,' said the Captain. 'And now you're up here, Chief, have a look at the ship from this angle. How many times have you been up here?'

Dundass coloured even more rufously. 'Indeed, sir, an' I've not been here since we built in Halifax itself. She's a very sturdy craft, I always say, sir, but I should like another ten feet astern,' and he saluted, and puffed his way below.

'And now, Number One,' said the Captain, 'you can get the leave rota out.'

'It's ready, sir,' I announced with precision. It had been ready a month, typed, and waiting for this very exquisite moment.

❦

I spent four days in London, thought I might journey to Wales for the last five days, but then deciding to take Dick Ives at his word, sent him a wire that I was coming, was it awkward? received 'far from awkward' as his reply and boarded a slow, mid-morning train from Liverpool Street to that small but extremely select East Coast holiday resort which, now deserted and its palmier times of cotton frocks and cricket weeks forgotten, sheltered instead several flotillas of MGBs and MTBs between the occasions of their North Sea excursions.

Dick met me at the station. Inevitably he was attended by his blonde Swedish wife. I knew Inga from peacetime days, and was not surprised to find that he had made it possible for her to live near the base. We had a lunch or unashamed nostalgic Solent reminiscence; I was then taken to my room in the hotel where the staff and officers of the MTB base were billeted.

'D'you feel fit enough to come out tonight or would you rather take Inga to the Wrens' dance?' Dick said as he showed me to my room, small, white, spotless.

These seemed unreasonable choices to thrust at me, and I was still puzzled by the nature of the formula which would enable me to travel as a spectator or passenger in this evening's proposed trip. 'Don't worry about that. Our Staff Officer, Intelligence, fixes all that. Last time I took out a Group Captain. All very inter-Service and all that. Surely we can take another naval type out.'

I wondered what the Director of the Anti-Submarine Warfare Division of the Admiralty would have to say if he knew.

'Shouldn't think he'd mind a bit. Very educational trip, you could say.'

I still wondered as Dick decided my fate, saying, 'Let's go out tonight and Inga can fix up a blonde WVS or Wren for you for tomorrow's dance – that's another given by the local ack-ack. We can make a foursome. We dine early, at six.'

~

About a dozen Sub-Lieutenants and Lieutenants, RN and RNVR, sat down to that early dinner. Conversation, if our chatter could be so dignified, was concerned mainly with the Wrens' dance which we were all missing. Somewhat presumptuously, it seemed, two of the sub-lieutenants were discussing the chagrin of the Wrens when they discovered that the better part of the Base's manhood had departed into warlike operations on the night of their dance. 'Base manhood, surely?' a youthful officer queried, but there was a loud groan at the heavy pun. Then, in defiance of all naval wardroom tradition, the qualities of the Wrens and their dance were analysed, with relative detachment, despite the attendance of the Wrens who served as stewards at the tables.

Differences in ages between officers were less marked than in wardrooms of trawlers and corvettes: there were youngsters of barely twenty but nobody nearer maturity than middle-aged creatures of thirty such as Dick and myself. I commented upon this. He agreed, but added that the wardroom held rather a miscellany. 'At first the powers-that-be were inclined to think that only the most headstrong and exuberant youths could command these mosquito craft with the necessary zip. Now, I believe they're prepared to admit that comparatively old men like myself have our moments.' Somebody spoke of the obvious gifts for any local spy which lay waiting in this very hotel, for always, before any operation, a lorry labelled RN arrived at a regular evening hour before the door and a group of young men clad in reefers, flannel slacks and seaboots, muffled often in heavy scarves and carrying oilskins, swung themselves upon the rickety coachwork and into the shadows of the back to sit sedately upon the side benches and then went off. 'Obviously not to a dance,' somebody added, almost bitterly.

Dinner was hurried: soup, steak and kidney pie, a chocolate mould and cheese. I wolfed my own meal and hoped I would not suffer later. Dick said that before his previous trip he had eaten lobster and had suffered grievously until he had come within sight of the Dutch coast and then things had become so lively that he had forgotten his supper and his sickness.

We rushed from the dining-room to the ante-room to swig our coffees. A petty officer came in to urge us to the waiting lorry.

The journey through the sedate, sunny streets was brief but bumpy. Voices within the van were speculative and anecdotal. At such times, underlying tension is apparent in the manner of the telling of tales and in too-quick, responding laughter. The lorry pulled into a gravelled yard before the Base offices and we tumbled out. The others went quickly through into the Operations Room where all the Captains and First Lieutenants were to be briefed.

I asked Dick whether he thought a visitor's interest could include listening to the briefing. In answer he took my arm and led me into a small room with a minute desk and essex-boarded walls covered with North Sea charts.

A dozen men were listening to a RN lieutenant outlining the night's projected programme. He was a fair, long-haired young man with a thin face and a lackadaisical manner; he was wearing the ribbons of the OBE and DSC. As Dick and I entered the room he was saying in a rather languid voice, 'I propose that we should go in here and see what we can see. One of our recce planes reported an enemy convoy this afternoon moving up towards the Dutch coast. I think we might try and spot them or any other convoy movements. If we get split up I think we ought to try to rendezvous about here,' and his dividers, which he had been moving casually before him as if he were a youthful ballet-master keeping time for a *pas deux*, moved precisely to the chart, making a fix. 'Please make a note of the position,' he said, and gave parallel and meridian from his chart. The First Lieutenants made notes. I supposed that they were, in all instances, the navigation officers. In corvettes the task usually fell to Number Two, although Number One in *Tobias* was always loth to let the navigation slip too far from his interest. 'It's fairly shallow there,' he continued, 'and I think any patrol craft will think twice about moving after us too closely. If there are any E-boats about we shall probably have our fun with them.' He continued his recital, giving directions, positions and times with clear definition. His languid voice, rather high-pitched, was, despite these qualities, incisive and authoritative. Listeners broke in from time to time: one to tell him that the state of the moon might be against a too-venturesome programme. The flotilla leader paused to consider the interruption and then agreed that perhaps he had been too optimistic, and returned to outline the earlier, more attractive part of his proposals: the hope that they might be able to attack the convoy already reported. He gave brief instructions concerning the manner of attack he proposed to make if things were propitious and the parts to be played by gunboats and torpedo-boats, the manner of their co-operation.

'Is everything quite clear now?' he asked at last. They nodded assent, and began to move from the room. I crossed the forecourt to the quay.

'What's the name of your flotilla leader?' I asked Dick.

'His name is Williams, but we call him Laurie, short for Laureate: because of his long locks. Can't say he's ever written any odes worth reciting. He's a good type.'

'How many craft in tonight's operation?'

'Six at the moment. Three MGBs, three MTBs. Two flotillas, but one of the MTBs is a bit dubious.'

A mighty roaring from many high-powered engines filled the earth. This cacophony was beyond anything I had ever heard. One could only talk by shouting to the full strength of one's lungs. I followed Dick across the decks of two MTBs holding the inner berths of the trot. Ratings lolled at their ease or sat upon superstructure: these moments were the engine-room's. All other tasks had been finished during the afternoon, Dick yelled, thinking I might think his mariners a lubberly lot. The men were very young, I noted, younger even than our own youthful ratings

An officer I had seen in the Operations Room poked his head from the Chart Room. 'John Ward, Number One,' called Dick, miming a movement of introduction. Dick yelled my name and we waved acknowledgments. The coxswain was young, about twenty-one, ten years younger than our own in *Tobias*. He had a rugged Spencer Tracy sort of profile and wore a battered petty officer's cap, a black oilskin suit, rubber shoes. About his neck he carried an impeccably laundered white silk square, obviously especially 'dhobeyed' for the evening's trip; I wondered whether this was a mannerism affected for each trip. The muffler was certainly decorative, but the wearer seemed unaware of such qualities; probably the warmth of silk was necessary to him in the cold night, but was such whiteness?

'Cast off!' called Dick; and the engines surged into greater noise, a primeval roar. We edged out slowly from the inner MTB, swung slowly into the small basin. The inner MTB, the flotilla leader chugged towards the outer harbour. The quayside seemed to tremble with movement and din; we saw the world through a haze of fumes. The crew seemed unaware of such afflictions. Number One clambered on deck. He said, shouting urgently at one-inch range, 'The Old Man likes us to stand to attention as we pass him at the jetty. Dick will salute. We stand like ramrods. The men try to.'

I obeyed the injunction. The Commander-in-Charge of the Base took our salutes, returned them. He had to do this to the six boats as they came out in line astern. It was a fairly long job. 'Not as tough as Stalin's May Day stuff,' said Number One, as he moved to go below to plot our course.

'Where d'you want me?' I asked.

'I con the ship and fire the fish from the starboard side. Coxswain takes the wheel. You'd better stay over there on the port side,' Dick said.

'Would I be more use forrard at one of the gun stations?' I asked.

'Good idea if any fun starts,' said Dick. 'We're always short of gunners. In fact, we're always short of everything when there's a real show.'

I looked round at the flotillas. We were moving at a speed of about eighteen knots and a sense of speed was beginning to be impressed upon my mind. The six craft with their sloped, swift lines, great crested bow waves and curdling wakes, thrilled the eyes. Against the coming dusk they seemed like twentieth-century, machine-age corsairs, as, indeed, some might have considered them.

Suddenly there was a commotion of hand-waving, signalling and megaphoning. Astern, the third MGB had stopped, now wallowed in the gentle waves. We stopped engines and also wallowed for five minutes, the beam motion a strange contrast to the planing motion of the boat at speed. The Captain of the MTB megaphoned that he would have to return to harbour with engine trouble. 'Tough luck!' yelled the flotilla leader, and then megaphoned to us that we would continue; our screws began to thread the water, and engines broke into their routine roar. Almost immediately afterwards I was deafened by a burst of gunfire astern and looking round saw the pom-pom going into action at one of the marking buoys. The gunner was grinning as he gave the buoy a miss in his practice shoot. Red and yellow tracers curved delicately above the swaying target. The noise was shattering at this distance of eight or nine feet and I glanced across to Dick: he was smiling and pointing to the cotton wool in his ears. Reminded thus of precautions I might reasonably have taken in order to lead as comfortable a life as possible, I remembered also that I was without oilskin, tin hat or lifebelt; that all these accoutrements of war and sea were safely in my cabin in *Tobias,* left behind in fond belief that I was taking leave of the ship for holiday and not for a venture of this sort. I went below to discuss the matter with Number One. He was unperturbed by such forgetfulness, equal to my requests. 'We always allow for one guest artiste,' he said. 'The tin hat may be awkward. You'd better take mine. If we run into fun I'm usually down below here. You can grab an oilskin from the wardroom and there's a gash lifebelt there.' He came through with me into the small, compact wardroom and routed out some venerable gear. I blew up the mae west: it looked mildly forlorn but quite useful. I missed the sense of abiding comfort which I always donned with the padded, kapok, life-saving waistcoat I had been given a year before by a torpedoed tanker officer we had picked up in the North Atlantic and deposited safely in Belfast. Such a waistcoat is not irreparably ruined in contact with a jagged spar: the thin rubber tubing of a mae west is more vulnerable; but my waistcoat was far away and there was an end to yearning. The oilskin was 'rather Ming' as Number One said and held to me by a solitary button, but it was an oilskin and I felt less naked against the night and possible bullets. 'Like to look at the chart?' asked Number One, 'and see the miracle of Coastal Forces at work?'

I said I would, interested to see how quickly a ship's position moved across a chart of narrow seas. It was unlike anything I had experienced, plotting a seven-knot convoy infinitesimally across the Atlantic; these computations would be more complicated, I thought.

'Not at all,' said Number One. 'I should think it's very much simpler. None of these damned deviations and variations changing every time you look at a chart.'

I asked whether he ever had occasion to use his knowledge of celestial navigation. He smiled, 'Never!' I smiled too, remembering Dick's letter, and that always, in *King Alfred,* prospective Coastal Forces officers had been the creatures who had been given the coveted three weeks' course in 'stars', never the prospective ocean mariners, who really needed every minute of instruction they could get before drafting.

'We work almost always on dead reckoning.' I made my protest about the idiocy of having given Dick and himself the course. 'Yes, I suppose it is rather crazy,' said the bland pilot.

'Rather an English way of doing things, don't you think? Anyway, it'll be jolly useful after the war for offshore racing.'

I clambered out of the chartroom and up to the bridge. Dusk had settled and the five boats rushed through the seas at a speed I judged to be near thirty knots. The world seemed much quieter: probably due to darkness. I was interested and relieved to find that the motion of the MTB was far more peaceful than that of a trawler or corvette. These mosquito craft planed through the sea rather like very fast hard-chine sharpies; there was a fair amount of pitching but virtually no beam roll and this has always been, for me at least, the most comfortable of all methods of seaways propulsion. I remembered vividly how often in *KA* the aged men of thirty had been told that their constitutions would not stand up to the racket and ardours of coastal craft. They had then been directed gently but firmly to the unholy, devastating roll of minesweepers or corvettes. Indeed, my stomach was more cosy than it had ever been at sea. I was prepared to concede that this was partly due to the fact that the sea was now as peaceful as Regent's Park lake, but *Tobias* always rolled, even on a summer's day in Bangor Bay.

A bright full moon drove a path across the sea, as sentimental a moon as any in a painting for a calendar. Only our phosphorescent wake disturbed the world. We went through the hours to midnight. They were short hours, for the faster a ship moves the faster time itself seems to be used: it was the sloth of convoys which gave such interminable monotony to hours in the Western Ocean.

Near midnight we were halted by the flotilla leader in the other MTB. The five ships stopped engines almost in line abreast: the flotilla commander addressed his small fleet by megaphone. He thought he had seen a ship on his starboard beam, and as he spoke three star shells burst high above us, directly ahead, and hung upon the night.

'Aha!' said Dick. 'Wondered when we'd have those chaps. They radar us quite easily.'

At such moments the world suddenly becomes poised upon eerie nightmare. Transition from daily, commonplace life at sea into the unreal life of war is swift, unragged.

'How near d'you think those are?' Dick said. I judged five to seven miles, not more.

'I make you about ten miles offshore,' said Number One, who had come on top.

'Wait, listen to old Laurie ...' hissed Dick, for the lieutenant was booming again through the megaphone. In the night his voice had a timbre of hardness: no trace of the lazy notes of the earlier evening remained. He said he thought he could see a craft of sorts: could anyone else?

We all peered. I could see only the broad roadway of the moon: no silhouette anywhere beyond.

The Laureate called the numbers of two gunboats. 'Go and have a look-see. I make it dead on my starboard beam.'

The roar of engines broke the quiet night again. We waited. Star shells rose and burst, searching the night and the sea.

In less than ten minutes the gunboats returned, having made a wide sweep to the east; they had seen 'nothing antagonistic,' a captain called.

'I still think I see the damned thing,' said the voice. He mapped out a plan for full inspection of the elusive enemy and then attack. 'OK?' he called finally. 'Let's go then.'

We moved off, gunboats leading, ourselves astern. After ten minutes we had still seen no ship. More star shells went up; the world was as brilliantly lit as peacetime Piccadilly.

'D'you think all these are from shore-based stuff?' yelled Number One, a dubious note in his voice.

'My money's still on shore,' shouted Dick. An aldis flash from the flotilla leader slowed our engines once more.

'Up a gum tree,' called the flotilla leader, 'Sorry, chaps.'

We hung about again. Then we saw the ships. Three lookouts must have spotted them in the same split second, for mingled words from the other boats moved across the water.

'I should think this is it,' said Dick, quietly.

I clambered forrard to the port gun. It seemed to be ready, but I was taking no chances and moved across the deck to the torpedo-rating closed up at the starboard gun.

'These are Lewis guns, aren't they?' I yelled. 'I've been used to Hotchkiss.'

'Yes, Lewis. The port gun's cocked and ready. Just press the trigger and if she jams keep pulling the cocking rod backwards and forwards. If it won't work then you've had it. Need a new barrel.'

Reassured, I crossed again to the gun.

We were increasing speed to something about twenty knots, when Dick yelled for me to come aft. I clambered back over the torpedo. 'We shan't need those at the moment,' he said after I had reached the bridge, 'and you'll have more fun up here. We're going in now.'

We watched the three MGBs streak off. Our speed had dropped again. The world misted, the big moon suddenly reticent within broken clouds. My eyes could not hold for long the wakes of the boats. Then tracers patterned the sky with their red, yellow and green criss-crossed streaks. These are the most strange moments of battle; it is almost impossible to realise that such patterns mean death. The gay parabolas are swift, exciting and pleasurable to the eyes; innocent-seeming, conjuring memories of bonfire nights in darkened gardens, certainly not thoughts of death.

'Who's the enemy?' I asked.

'Flak patrol, I should think,' said Dick. 'Four trawlers, I count. Maybe a south-bound convoy. Don't seem to be any E-boats about.'

The exchanges between the gunboats and the German 'flak' patrol, probably stiff with oerlikons and the enemy equivalent of our own four-inch guns, were lively, fierce. There was a sense of schoolboy innocence about the whole thing, rather like two sparring boys dodging around each other.

'This is where we go in,' yelled Dick. Our speed was still uncomfortably moderate, I thought, watching over the bridge as we came into their range. Tracer always seems so easy to dodge. Streams of gay colours come from out of the darkness ahead, quietly, quietly, slowly, slowly and then are suddenly here, coming in curves not swift enough to strike, too colourful to kill. I ducked beneath the bridge, and then came up again, forgetting that between the obvious tracers were those many invisible shells, not following quite the same marked course. We were hit twice forrard: the hits were obvious, seeming to splay into the ship between wind and water, and the cracks were unmistakable. The enemy's fire seemed quite accurate. We went steadily forward, speed increasing. I kept poking my tin hat above the bridge and taking a peek. The coxswain seemed to be dodging some of the tracers that had him in a dead line: he was crouched against his steering wheel, almost flat against the bridge. Dick was hunched as tightly as he could get himself inside his oilskin whilst still retaining complete control of the ship; I could see him adjusting the sights to get his torpedo in line with his target and fingering the release mechanism.

'Hold her now,' he yelled. I looked up and over. We were going straight for what I judged a silhouette of a large trawler. She seemed to be firing from several guns. The night was noisier and we were criss-crossed with tracers. Probably another ship had joined in, too, I thought. Shells seemed to be reaching us more quickly than a minute since. Dick yelled above the racket 'Can't make!' and then 'Hard aport!'

We went round on his words, the helmsman using the small wheel ferociously as if in frenzy.

As we came round tracers began to get us from the quarter. This was more disturbing, for we were now wide open. The metalled base of the revolving gun turret amidships gave us some protection, but not much. I was suddenly aware of the very wide gap through which shells might get us. Then they were coming in from dead astern. I stepped aft and heard two smacks against the turret ricochet off. The craft seemed to be going all out but the German gunners were keeping the increasing range extraordinarily well.

'Think we've been hit,' called Dick.

'I know we've been hit,' I said very firmly.

'Now we'll go in and get the so and so,' I heard him yell, but the yell was mainly for his own benefit, I thought.

We came round again in a wide sweep to port.

'I'm going for the same bastard again,' Dick shouted to his coxswain. 'Keep her steady on the run in, Rogers. Couldn't get a bead that time.' We proceeded slowly again, as if to an invisible starting line, so slowly that I became impatient. I had no job and merely watched, fidgeting, hating the excessively careful job we seemed to be making of the approach, knowing that it was the sharp contrast between this speed and our precipitate retreat that gave such an impression of sloth to my mind.

We had the same reception. It was interesting to expect and to note the speeding-up of the tracer as we came in. This was one way of passing the time. Then suddenly we seemed very close. Surely he'll let it go now, I thought in agony, and watched for the wake of the torpedo, but Dick waited another hundred or hundred and fifty yards and then the torpedo left us with a deep, urgent swish. 'Hard astarboard,' Dick said sharply, 'and let's get the hell out of here.' We swung round in a concentrated arc, getting their fire again. I counted three thuds and wondered where they had hit us.

'Missed, dammit,' said Dick, and I saw he was looking at a luminous stop watch. 'In we go again,' and he ducked from flak that the trawler was sending in from astern.

We came round.

We went in again, closer this time: so close that I thought that Dick had gone suddenly berserk and decided that we might turn the evening into a cutting-out expedition. We went into about five hundred yards, carefully, steadily. The coxswain was apparently getting used to this as routine for the evening, it seemed, for he was as steady as an old, old salt. 'Now!' yelled Dick and fired and came round again on a starboard escape. The trawler was still firing. We seemed to have lost all contact with the others of our fleet. The MGBs had disappeared: the other MTB was nowhere to be seen. This had become an affair between ourselves and the trawler, or so it seemed to me, but I was ignorant of this sort of warfare. 'One of the gunboats kept him busy. Good old Buster, I'll bet,' said Dick, and in that moment we heard the dulled explosion. 'Think that's us,' said Dick. 'Thought I couldn't miss that time.' I looked astern. The flak ship was massed smoke and steam. There were no flames. The battle seemed still to be joined, but the tracers were fewer and more sporadic.

We steadied on our course, and seemed to be out of intensive shelling. Then suddenly we were hit three times in a new burst that found us, accurately, viciously. In a moment a great cloud of steam and fumes rolled up from the engine-room, curling heavily around the gun turret.

'What's going on,' shouted Dick as our speed began to drop alarmingly. Then we were stopped. Number One came up with a clatter. 'For Christ's sake, John, find out what's going on aft!' A man came forrard through the maze, choking in a ghastly way and fell on the deck, amidships, out. Another man said, 'Three hits in the engine-room, sir. Gone through the pipes.'

The engine-room petty officer came along the deck. He seemed to be moving very slowly and gingerly, I thought, as I stepped down from the bridge to see what could be done about the man who had crumpled. As my feet touched the deck I slipped. I grabbed a fire extinguisher from the port side of the bridge as I almost went overboard in a wild skid. I came to a solid stop against part of the superstructure. 'Mind how you go, sir,' cried the petty officer. 'They put a shell into a ten-gallon drum of oil we had on deck.'

'Why have it on deck?' snapped Dick.

I handed the extinguisher to the petty officer and followed him aft, stepping like a nonagenarian on an iced pond. Immediately fumes swirled around us and we began to cough. I fumbled for a handkerchief and stuffed it in my mouth, and bent down over the rating. He seemed in a bad way. I ripped away a muffler from his neck, tugged him forrard over the slippery deck. Clouds of steam and gas were still moiling up the engine-room hatchway. Somebody wearing a respirator poked a macabre head above the deck and took the extinguisher.

We were beginning to wallow from side to side, quite helpless. A rating said, 'Let me, sir,' and took over the casualty, trying energetic artificial respiration. I hoped he might have sick berth training and returned to the bridge, not anxious to be in the way.

The ship which ten minutes before had been a spick and span minor man-o'-war was now a shambles. Thick oil ran greasily about the deck. Below me were the two ratings, one working the arms of his unconscious shipmate. Number One was aft. I saw him vaguely through the smoke, standing above silhouettes that disappeared into the engine-room or came from that hell-hole. Dick still conned the ship, anxious, taut.

Only the gunner, enclosed within his glass-domed turret, seemed calm, remote from this turmoil. He gazed down at the chaos like a benign deity, but I doubted whether he was as calm as he appeared; but he had a job, dividing his regard between the enemy and our own melee.

More star shells went up, and, with the moon, made a distressing brightness of the night. I had a sinking feeling in the stomach and considerable despair, not due solely to our undignified plight, for I had a very clear picture of Willoughby's cold fury had he known that his Number One was engaged in this sort of excursion. I could expect no sympathy from him that I should now be wallowing about in a helpless MTB ten miles off the Dutch coast, quite cooked. That I knew.

One of the enemy ships evidently saw us and began to send over tracer again, but we were perhaps a hundred yards out of range. 'Damn, damn, damn,' said Dick. 'How long, Number One. God, God, God.'

'Can't tell, sir. Getting the fire under control and patching the pipes.'

'So we're on fire, too, are we?' said Dick, laconic, resigned. 'Wonder where the others are?'

The battle continued; mainly, we judged, between the gunboats and the trawlers, but we spared few thoughts or glances for comrades. Our own mess seemed complete enough.

We waited through what seemed a slice of eternity. I had time to speculate upon the folly of this excursion: how impossible it would be to explain that I was really not to blame if I were killed or captured and only then realised the folly of such speculations: I should be very far removed from any inquiry. Only these vivid recollections come back to me from that time. How strange, I think now, that at such a moment I should be so fearful of authority. These fears alternated, I remember, with a comforting relief that I had no wife and family to brood upon my absence. I suppose those with families find relief in the belief that they will be brooded upon. Each of us makes his own escape.

'All right now, sir,' called Number One.

'Make it snappy, then. We're drifting near those bloody Heinies again,' said Dick. He was watching the enemy, the battle and his ship.

The unconscious rating was recovering under the forceful methods of his mate. Hope began to rise again. Once more the lively egoism of man began to believe again in his own essential immortality.

In less than five minutes our engines swung over and began to churn the North Sea into foam. Life and voice recovered in the strained ship.

'Let's push off,' said Dick: 'I'm going straight back. Think old Laurie would approve.' We moved away from the rabble which seemed almost over. At something under ten knots we moved westwards. We were not yet out of danger, but no soul on board believed that harm could reach us now. Such very famous last words and beliefs!

❧

We had one other scare on the way back. A squally dawn was splitting the world at about 0430 hours when a German plane passed directly over us, going at such great speed, flying very low, that we had no time to give an alarm.

'Probably didn't see us,' said Dick. 'Thank God he didn't, anyway. We're in no shape to take on a Heinkel right now.'

I felt very tired, very hungry. We had coffee and baked beans on toast. I would be able to go straight off to sleep, said Dick longingly, but he would have to write up the blasted log and a brief report.

❧

The others were back when we arrived and had waited about the quay against our return. The flotilla leader met Dick at the quayside ladder. They had torpedoed one of the trawlers. 'I was a bit worried, old boy, but old Buster said he'd seen you limp off. He came and looked for you and then pushed home. Did you enjoy the trip?' he asked me.

I said I had, with reservations.

'These corvette types get rather settled in their ways,' said Dick, explaining all, and, in solace, 'Still you brought us luck. Best show we've had in months.'

'I wonder whether you thought so four hours ago,' I said in speculation.

'Now don't get peevish, old boy. Let's go and have breakfast.'

I went back in the lorry and straight to my hard, iron, naval-pattern bed, and slept as if on clouds until lunch-time. Afterwards, with Inga and with Dick, I walked the forsaken, derelict sea-front of the town. Small boarding houses, sandbagged against menace from the sea, were falling into jagged, dirty ruins. A few housewives and unemployed landladies with shopping baskets and prams, stood at corners and talked. Troops of the Royal Army Service Corps and a few ack-ack gunners drank tea within the bare rooms of semi-detached, seaside villas 'overlooking the front'. Empty cafés and olde Englishe tea shoppes gaped upon the empty esplanade. It was a sunny, early autumn day, saddening in its inevitable summoning of memories from the years of peace.

I noticed these things, listening to Inga's chatter about the coming evening's dance and to Dick's gallant indulgence of his wife's engaging difficulties with the English language. The contrast with the previous evening's entertainment would doubtless be marked, said Dick, and when Inga queried, 'Why, Dickie?' he said, 'Because, my dear, tonight we shall be face to face with all the man-eating Wrens and ATS of this man-eating base, infinitely more dangerous than anything

that Adolf has yet spawned.' Inga laughed: seeming to have
no fear of man-eating Wrens where 'Dickie' was concerned.

❧

Two days later, in the train going north, I read in *The Times* a
short note about our evening. Other, more popular newspapers
dealt with the incident of our modest battle and with the
flotilla leader's remarkable night vision rather more luridly,
but the prose of Printing House Square was considered, calm,
almost academic. Under the heading of SHARP EYESIGHT
IN THE DARK – SUCCESSFUL ACTION BY COASTAL
FORCES, that augustan journal gave a brief account of the
encounter, but the Naval Correspondent seemed anxious to
get to the much more interesting point that the senior officer
had sighted the *flak* patrol at a range of four miles. He pointed
out that 'some people are endowed by nature with sharper
eyesight than others, but it is not an unusual phenomenon for
responsibility to stimulate the power of observation. Many
naval officers have noticed that objects of interest at sea,
particularly in the dark or in low visibility are very frequently
sighted by the officer on whom the responsibility for action
will rest, before they are reported by lookouts.'
'Nuts,' I said aloud, remembering my own somewhat
lackadaisical powers of vision, and annoyed that the naval
correspondent should give seven lines to the Laureate's
eyesight and four lines to the fire on board our craft.

❧

'Have a decent leave?' asked Willoughby as I went into his
cabin to report back from leave. 'Any excitements?'
    'A few German bombs,' I said.
    'Didn't you go to Wales, then?'

'Too far and too many people to see in London,' I answered. 'How nice to be the popular social type!' he said, handing me a signal. 'Now you can go and be social to that velvet-arsed signal officer sitting on his fat hunkers in that old crock of a cruiser and ask what he means by telling us to be in all respects ready for war by tomorrow morning ten o'clock, when he knows damn well we don't get a clearance from the bloody port plumber until midday.'

Once again I knew I had come home.

❧

A month later, over waffles and maple syrup in the *Green Lantern* in Halifax, I showed Willoughby the paragraph torn from *The Times*. He read it through. After my denial that I was trying to be funny about his eyesight, he queried its significance. I explained my diffident part in the evening's pleasures.

'Jolly good idea,' he said. 'Often thought I'd like an evening out in one myself. Glad I didn't have to go looking for a new Number One. What sort of wardroom have they got?'

We talked MTBs the rest of the meal. One could never tell how our Captain would react to anything.

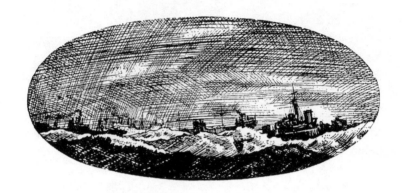

Chapter 8

Farewell to *Tobias*

The return to the long round voyages of the Western Ocean convoys held no attraction for us after the respite of our boiler-clean, although there was satisfaction, as always, in leaving the routine of the port and those inevitable daily contacts (and sometimes clashes) with the Staff Officers, for whom, unjustifiably enough, we had no great affection. For one or two experts who came aboard we had nominal, almost hearty salutations, but there were others who in Willoughby's words, 'littered the place like a pack of pekes', but bitter words have always been used by more active creatures of those who serve and sit. Some of the staff officers undoubtedly had difficult jobs, but many of them certainly had not, and seemed to keep hours as comfortable as a bank clerk's, put on airs and graces and wandered ashore each night to the Grand Central looking as nautical as hard cases out of a Jack London novel. The Base asdic and degaussing officers, however, we held in especial esteem when they clambered on board. Despite their green stripes, they were workmen and, even more important, we thought, our own lives might depend some time in the future upon their technical efficiency on board *Tobias;* so, after their inspections, examinations, tinkerings and advice, we escorted them to the wardroom with the Captain's usual farewell, 'What about a noggin?', and invariably the cloth was being laid for our midday meal before they clambered over the side to take their own lunch in the Missions to Seamen shanty, staffed by two clergymen and pretty Belfast girls who served up sausages, bacon and eggs with much gay banter in soft Ulster voices.

Sometimes we went ourselves to the Mission, lured perhaps by the Northern Irish air or soft voices or fresh eggs, or even perhaps by a sense of piety by proximity or proxy. There we met many officers from the trawlers, for they found the provender rather better than anything their own galleys and stewards could produce. We went to learn the gossip of the port, for that was the only place where we could learn anything of the Battle of the Atlantic, apart from the out-of-date paragraphs we read in ancient newspapers. One or two of the Staff Officers gave us information from the Admiralty Weekly Intelligence Report; sometimes we had that journal delivered to us. For its contents and details we were grateful; it is well known that those engaged in battles know less of the battle than the spectator or the historian, but sometimes we thought we heard and knew too little, and Mission gossip was poor substitute for truth. Once again Willoughby's thought, that each port should have a War Room, accessible to ships' officers, showing the state of the Battle of the Oceans, seemed to have the point of necessity about it. 'We should scarcely be likely to go and spill any beans and they needn't put all the secret dope on the damned thing,' he once said, after a rumour of many sinkings. 'I don't want to know where the

Queen Mary is at any given moment, but I should like to know that we're not losing the battle,' and many of us thought the same.

We did not go often to the Mission, however, for Jake Gibbs, although nominally steward, was too good a cook for us to wish to leave his table for very long, and in port he excelled even his own legendary ocean meals, taking full advantage of the ample stores which the naval victualling yards distributed as if to atone for early traditions of weevilled biscuits and salt beef. He had other sources, too, and into these we did not inquire too curiously, telling ourselves that Ulster was rich farming country, anyway, and that chickens were indigenous and probably not in short supply, and thus sat down to soup, fried chicken and French fried potatoes, runner beans and then chocolate trifle without a questioning word. Only at the end did Willoughby sometimes comment, saying slyly, 'That was a notable meal, Jake. Perhaps you have a girl friend working on a Derry farm?'

'Perhaps I have, sir,' said Jake, unsmiling, and then with a huge, slow wink, 'And what time breakfast in the morning, sir? Grapefruit, bacon and eggs, sir?'

Did such thing happen in pukka service ships? we sometimes wondered.

❧

At sea, autumn storms came once more into our lives and I did not like them. Still my stomach could not become attuned to the mighty swells and even mightier sloughs into which *Tobias* seemed destined one day to disappear. Yet I was not in so bad a way as I had been the year before. Now I could withstand the shock as we heeled or stood upon our beam ends, but I still spent too much time whilst off watch lying flat in my bunk considering the white-painted steel plates above my head, sickened of the unlovely world yet never to the point of sickness. How many letters remained unwritten because I dared not move from bunk. How many official forms remained uncompleted. How many calls to meals I left unanswered. Sea-sickness varies, as all the world knows; Willoughby once contended that my variation was perhaps the worst, for I could never claim relief in actual sickness. Perhaps he was right, but in union with all other mariners I could not bear to think that I might prove so weak that I might miss a watch, and found unholy pride in persistence, yet always as my time of watch drew near, I looked frequently and furtively at my wrist, watching the seconds pass, dreading the sojourn of the succeeding hours. At twenty minutes to the hour I climbed from the bunk like an aged man, to pull on slacks, reefer, short seaboots and oilskin. I acquired a formula for the procedure, in the manner of a man who, having tested many methods of slitting his throat, finds, at last, the least painful. I dressed almost fully whilst still seated upon a chair wedged firmly between the bunk and the small desk, even placing my cap upon my head whilst still seated and still bootless. (The ritual would perhaps have made a successful music-hall performance in the Grock tradition, as Willoughby once said, but I was never sufficiently enthused to wish to try.) Finally there was the moment of getting on the half-Wellington rubber boots. This I did by lowering my arms, seizing and placing the boot upon my toes, placing the boot firmly against a bulkhead and ramming it thus upon my foot, daring not to bend lest the queasiness within my empty stomach might prove too much, and yet I knew it never would.

Then I arose, in almost all respects ready for war.

Hours upon the bridge were more painful, for there we stood or paced the narrow span, and the only temporary relief that I could gain was to stand close to the hand-rail built around the inside of the bridge-house. This hand-rail was just too low to fit snugly across my stomach, but by bending slightly at the knees the rail fitted firmly and comfortingly against me, and the pressure seemed to brace the walls of my stomach, to restore some sense of security within my body. In the darkness of the night hours I was persuaded that nobody could see my remedy and I behaved in a manner demanded of an officer of the watch. During daylight watches I used my method of evasion only at dire moments, yet in that had folly, for if anyone had noted my posture it would have gone unremarked. Everyone on board had been sick at one time or another, and for seamen, in any case, sea-sickness is part of a daily, common lot and they are thus far less concerned about admitting to the malady than other folk, who seem to regard assertions concerning their freedom from sea-sickness as a point of honour, and sea-sickness as a shame to be hidden in pride, but perhaps I have written overmuch upon this sorry personal digression: I will return to my tale.

Yet the tale itself is almost as sorry. Sometimes I was inclined to agree with the ratings I heard chanting some of the doggerel couplets which, unwritten and unprinted, made their way through the ships of the Fleet as if by bush telegraph. Untunefully, as they moved about their watch below, they sang their dirge:

> Roll on the *Nelson*, the *Rodney*, the *Hood*
> These two-funnelled bastards are no bloody good
> And this single-stack bastard we're rolling in now
> Ain't much bloody better, the bloody old cow.

Hearing the men chanting the monotonous words I wished that the scribbling Admiralty creature who had written that officers must 'check all profane swearing and improper language' might be listening. I should have welcomed his advice on procedure, or even alternatives for the recurring words. Swear words were varied to choice, but the sentiments remained steadfast and the voices of many who served in corvettes would have risen wholeheartedly to swell the chorus. The storms that autumn seemed unending, or perhaps we were unlucky in the routes we were given. Always we seemed destined to zig-zag our way steadily into a cyclone, anti-cyclone or simple old-fashioned hurricane. There was no comfort in our frequent assertions and deceptions that 'this weather would keep the Hun down'. I had an almost greater loathing of the elements than of the Germans. Each trip dragged out into a third week and tempers about the ship could not stand against continuing sleeplessness and soakings. There was never respite or relief. Men went off wet watches to wet mess-decks. Small electric heaters could not dry out socks, vests, shirts, sweaters that had been relentlessly sodden for four hours on an open bridge or on a gun platform. Men had no wish to change and could not. Even the handkerchiefs they sometimes raised to wipe the rain from their faces were as wet and grimed as dishcloths, and I knew that they often stood their watches with rain and sea in equal measure in their seaboots, down their necks.

Yet even in their misery their sardonic philosophy did not leave them. Said one to his relief:

'Why I stay in this bleeding ship I can't think. I was just thinking: if I was to go overboard I wouldn't be any wetter, I wouldn't 'ave to stand any more bleeding watches and it'd soon be over.'

'Why don't you do it then?'

'Dunno. It's probably all this money the Navy pays me. What's on below? Turkey? Roly-poly?'

'Same old spudoosh.' (Their title for the dish of potatoes, stew, and anything remotely edible that cook could put into a galley-pot.)

197

Another exchange between a lookout and his relief on a night of unrelenting, vertical sleet and visibility nil:

'Bloody awful night.'

'Don't get any better, do it?'

A pause.

'Why d'you join the Navy, chum?'

'Dunno, really. To see the world, I suppose.'

'Seen much of it?'

'Not much. Seen a lot o' water, though.'

'Gets on yer nerves, don't it?'

'Suppose it does. Still, I'd rather 'ave sea than sand.'

'Why?'

'Christ knows. Suppose it's cos I never liked gettin' sand in me boots when I was a kid.'

'Did yer like gettin' water in yer boots then?'

'You got me there, chum. Wonder why I did join the Navy, anyway?'

'I'll tell yer why.'

'Why?'

'Cos yer bleedin' daft.'

'Praps you're right.'

'Cos I'm right. Goodnight.'

'Goodnight, chum.'

❧

We seemed unable to escape from this confinement of despair. Day and night were occupied with the monotony of buffeting and smashing seas. In the daytime we could watch the merchantmen and tankers taking heavy beatings, and always had compassion for men in the heavily-loaded tankers. Great seas caught their bows, and then crashed and ran along the open expanse of their decks, uncluttered by normal superstructure. Nothing impeded the volume and weight of water, and we sometimes watched in wonder as great seas swirled along the decks, submerging them completely because of their low freeboard and great cargoes of oil. At such times only the bows and the bridge of a tanker seemed to protest and fight against the hundreds of massed tons of the Atlantic hurled upon the ship; only those parts of the ship could be seen. The rest was drowned and it seemed that nothing built of iron and steel could have buoyancy enough within itself to rise again and live.

Sometimes we saw small figures of officers clamber down from the bridge and bend their way against the wind along the gangways which ran both sides of tankers, peering down upon the hatches, striving to make their observations between the waves: always, through our glasses, we could see the masters on their bridges, stolid, immovable creatures, seemingly without relief. They probably were, for many, we heard, never left their bridges between Halifax and the Clyde or Avonmouth, and we came to believe this tale, for on each voyage we quickly knew the silhouettes of the merchantmen and tankers we escorted and through the glasses our eyes could never find the shapes of some skippers absent from their bridges.

The tasks and trials and dangers of tankermen we placed above our own. At that time they were perhaps the biggest prizes that could fall to Nazi U-boat commanders; it was not until a later period in the Atlantic Battle that the U-boats began to work to instructions that they should try to destroy the escort vessels before they set upon the merchantmen.

I had learned in *Solander* something of the way of life of these other men who sailed in these convoys and of whom we had had, before the war, so slight a knowledge. Officers we had picked up from a torpedoed tanker had talked. That was a year before: now we were to have a similar but grimmer experience, for on the second of our trips in that autumn we ran into trouble.

An unreasonable storm which we had endured halfway across the Atlantic dropped when we were about eight hundred miles from Ireland. Relief came with cessation of the gale, but we knew that now perhaps we should have other tribulations.

'I think I'd rather have storms any day or night than the prospect of these Heinies,' said Willoughby, as I came on watch for his relief.

I could scarcely agree, for this was the first day in almost ten that I had been able to rise to eat my food like a man and not nibble like a mouse.

'I know all that,' said the Captain, 'but look at that!' and his arm swept round, almost in an oratorical manner, to include the convoy sailing serenely under ominous, but containing clouds. 'This is the first time since leaving Halifax that we've seen the whole bloody convoy and as soon as that happens you can bet your last ha'penny there'll be trouble.'

Trouble came that night. We did not become involved beyond a call to action stations and a call from the senior escort, a destroyer, to keep with the convoy on the port beam, and keep a close-range asdic sweep. This we did, and in the morning received a signal that we should keep a lookout for survivors.

The day came up fierce and the anti-cyclone we thought we had escaped came once more to darken our lives. All through that day we made no more than ten miles upon our ocean passage. We could sight three out of thirty ships and hoped that each of the other escorts might account for as many, but it was doubtful. Waves lifted us to great heights and smashed us down. We thought upon our signal, gave up the survivors and dreaded the coming night.

Yet in the night we came upon them in one of those unaccountable meetings which only the vagaries of the ocean make accountable. We had made ten miles, and the cockleshell of a lifeboat had made as few, perhaps more. In the black night we saw small stabs of light, now momentarily seen but immediately quenched by the night and the great waves.

The Captain, on the bridge (where he had been for three days and nights), accepted the urgent message in the lookout's battering upon the bridge-house window and pointing arm, and went out on to the bridge. I went with him.

'A light, he says, Number One.'

I could not believe it possible, yet in a moment it came again, and again was lost beneath a wave.

'We'll try to edge this damned old tub over there,' said Willoughby. He gave five degrees starboard, then another five. Between the movements the ship took one wave that threatened to crack her welded plates apart, but round she came and the light had nearness.

'How a ship's lifeboat can live in this, I can't think,' yelled Willoughby.

At such a distance and in such a night I thought it impossible that we could be seen, but eyes within the boat must have been sharp, awake, for the torch began to stab out a message, yet still we could not see the outline of the craft, and there was always the danger that we might run her down, but our searchlight's beam sprayed suddenly within the night, falling in fitful effort upon the sea as the operator began to search the closer world. Voices called instruction and direction. Their small sounds, strained by the wind, came but faintly to the bridge.

Then the beam quivered suddenly upon the boat. 'Just like one of those blasted drawings in the *Illustrated London News*,' said Alphabet by my side.

I was amused by the aptness of his comment; as usual, his mind, with its continuous plying for strange and oblique images, had resolved and found the picture which had hovered nebulously deep within one's own mind. How strange had life indeed become when it gained greater reality in being likened to a second-hand depiction of life.

Half an hour later we had all the men aboard, and in the modest recital of one of the ship's officers, words from weekly intelligence reports were quickened, became alive.

'I managed to get into one of the boats, God knows how,' he said. 'I was turned in. Had most of my cabin door blown on top of me. One of the falls had been carried away and the damned thing was hanging by the after fall. Most of the others had been blown into the sea and half the ship on top of 'em. Christ knows how any of them stayed alive. Some didn't, I know. My arm had been crocked by the cabin door and I got hurt again by being thrown into the boat's bottom. The lifeboat was a complete shambles. The ship was beginning to settle and there was a hell of a bloody sea running. I got a knife and managed to cut the painter. Not so easy with the wrong hand and things a bit awkward-like. We went down like a sack o' coal and hit the sea as if we'd fallen a thousand feet. Never thought we'd make it, but we did, although we came up full of water. We started baling. I could see some of the others in the sea around us but we were out of control and drifted away. They all had these life jackets,' and he pointed to his own with the small light attached, 'so I think they could be seen and I believe a couple of the other lifeboats earlier away could have reached 'em. We drifted round under the stern of the ship. She seemed to have stopped sinking, but you can't be certain about these things at such times. By that time I didn't much care. The First Engineer was in the boat with me and he had been badly injured and scalded down in the engine-room when we were hit. There were thirteen of us, more dead than alive. Finally we got her clear of the ship and got some of the water out of the boat. Then the Chief collapsed. I don't think he died then. I got the others rallied a bit, but we were all shaken and moved like a lot of damned dolls. You'd give a chap an order and he couldn't do anything, just sit staring at you from the bottom of the boat. Anyway, we got the oars working and picked up two chaps in the drink. By this time it was dawn, but there was such a sea running that we couldn't see anything or anybody, certainly nothing of the rest of the convoy. About seven we thought we saw our ship go down, but we only caught a sight between the waves. They must have been thirty to fifty feet high. I think the fact we were so dumb probably saved us. If we'd tried to work the boat we'd have sunk ourselves, sure as fate. So we just lolled about and the boat went up with one sea, down with the next. We were all sick and there was a good deal of blood about. About midday I began to recover a bit and took a look at the First Engineer, but he was dead. Then I thought I ought to try to get things going. My arm was still groggy but we had a look at the stores. Most of the water had gone and the biscuits were half sodden as usual, but we had some condensed milk and some malted milk tablets. So we fed ourselves and began to perk up. I fixed watches. I think it was a good thing we didn't have to pull. We kept three watches going at the tiller and here we are.'

'Here we are' seemed too simple a peroration for the tale, covering too easily the intervening hours of misery and despair. Yet it was easy enough to imagine the horror of that boat, with fourteen half-dead men and one dead, adrift in an Atlantic storm. 'I just don't know how they lived through it,' said Willoughby. 'Yet I suppose it's always happened and always will. Not a single logical reason in the world why they should be here and here they are.'

'Perhaps a future prime minister is amongst them,' said Alphabet blandly.

Willoughby, very tired, grinned. 'I didn't know you were such a romantic, Benson,' he said.

'My mother was that way inclined,' said Benson. Neither horror nor storm could repress his determination to be facetious at all costs. Now, as in most cases, his manner gave us all the safety-valve we needed. Perhaps he knew that.

❧

These were experiences within our own ken, before our own eyes, but upon the ocean, at all times we knew that men were adrift and dying, survivors and losers in the Atlantic Battle. In the Weekly Intelligence Reports which came from the Admiralty we were able to read the sober background to the Battle: lists of convoys, arrivals, sinkings and impressive totals of tonnages discharged, records of attacks. Perhaps we gained some sense of detachment in the laconic paragraphs:

The *Pall Mall*, 2,448 tons, under Government Charter, independently routed from Aberdeen, was bombed by aircraft 15 miles north of Kinnaird Head on May 16th and severely damaged. She has, however, been beached north of Aberdeen and 99 casualties, including 12 dead, have been landed at Peterhead and Aberdeen.

The *Doomsday*, 7,939 tons, homeward bound from New Orleans, was bombed and sunk by Focke Wulf aircraft about 213 WNW of the Bloody Foreland on May 17th. One officer was killed and 50 survivors were landed at Londonderry.

The *Regency*, 5,444 tons, was torpedoed on July 4th about 600 miles West by South of the Canary Islands. She was bound from London to Capetown and Beira with a general cargo and had been in Convoy OB337. Nothing is at present known about the fate of her crew.

It is now known that the *Richmond Gem*, 7,628 tons, was torpedoed and sunk by a submarine on June 7th about 500 miles south-west of the Cape Verde Islands. Thirteen of the crew were drowned, one man died in the boat and 32 survivors were landed at Capetown.

The lists continued, each cool paragraph containing an unwritten record of horror and courage. We read them always with interest, looking always for the names of vessels we had escorted or had encountered in the Atlantic ports. Sometimes, too, the reports contained accounts of experiences whilst adrift, written by survivors, and for a while such notes as 'thirteen of the crew were drowned, one man died in the boat', were quickened by the modest prose of a ship's officer.

The grimmest record was of the sinking of a liner earlier in the year. An officer's letter to his wife was printed with her permission. Willoughby passed it over to me whilst we were in port and I was sitting in his cabin. 'You might like to read this, Number One; it's not exactly pleasant but the prose is Defoe. Hope we don't have a similar experience to write up one of these days.' I read the account later in my own cabin. The liner had been sunk in mid-South Atlantic, 700 miles west of Freetown, and the writer, an officer on passage, had been adrift for days in a lifeboat with three other naval officers, also on passage, six ratings, one of the ship's officers, a ship's gunner, a stewardess, and thirty-seven Lascars and Indians.

The boat's fresh water supply had been destroyed, and biscuits were saturated with salt water. The boat could not be pulled or sailed because of its waterlogged condition. The letter continued: 'We were without a rudder, and were forced to use an oar over the stern to keep the boat head on to wind and swell which was rather heavy. Meanwhile other boats were making sail in a manner which made our position seem more hopeless. The sun was terrific, and there was no way of sheltering from it. Then we discovered 48 small tins of condensed milk. The officers held a council to decide the best method of using them, the decision being to use three tins a day to be shared by the whole of the company. By puncturing the tin with two holes each one was allowed one suck each per tin. In this manner we managed to live and worked the boat for five days and five nights. The natives did no work, could not be trusted, and so the officers did not sleep or even doze during this time, which was spent in managing the boat and looking for a ship to pick us up. The need for water soon made itself apparent, and we warned everyone of the dangers of touching salt water, but soon the desire to drink was too much for some of them; they drank salt water, wanted more and then went mad until they eventually died. Our ship sank on Tuesday morning. On Wednesday three natives died, and we threw the bodies overboard. This brought the horrible sharks round our boat in ever-increasing numbers. Every day we tried to bale the water from the boat but it was impossible owing to the swell and shell holes. Once we got the water down six inches after two hours' work, and while resting to get our breath and strength back, which was fast ebbing, a huge wave came over and filled the boat again; it was indeed very heartbreaking. On Thursday fifteen people died. We could not read a burial service over them, but reverently removed our caps and helmets when committing them to the deep. On Friday eighteen more went mad and died. The sights were indeed pitiful, and I cannot put them down on paper sufficiently clear to describe them. All this time we tried to keep an iron grip on ourselves, not only for our own good but for the good and morale of the remaining survivors. Many times it seemed as though rain would fall but though we prayed hard it never came. Two or three times during the night some would suffer from delusions and walk over the side to what they thought was a hotel or public house where they could get drinks. It was on Friday night that the stewardess after a valiant attempt to live, went mad and died. She was a woman of 50 who had already lost her husband at sea. On Saturday afternoon six more went mad and died, and we settled down that night with eight remaining survivors of the original fifty. At about 6.45pm someone croaked "A light". We had heard that before; this time, however, it was true, and we lit our flares which were lashed to the mast to keep them dry. Soon a searchlight was sweeping the ocean and after about an hour we were sighted and rescued in an exhausted condition, having passed away five days and four nights in conditions beyond description, but praying all the time, having faith in our ultimate rescue. The liner that rescued us was Spanish. Actually there were only seven survived out of fifty in my boat, the one remaining coloured man dying just as we were sighted. The seven were, including myself, four officers and three ratings. I used to imagine how difficult it would be to die,' concluded the writer, 'but now I know how easy it is and how much one must struggle and have faith to live.'

Another record told in mildly facetious understatement of a stupendous task carried out at night in the North Atlantic. An armed merchant cruiser had been torpedoed and caught fire. Half the crew had got away from the burning ship: the others had crowded together aft, for no boats or Carley floats remained. A destroyer had therefore gone alongside again and again so that the men might leap from their ship to the destroyer. A gale had been blowing, waves were between fifty and sixty feet high. No destroyer could have survived a collision with such a ship of such tonnage, and in such an operation a collision would have seemed inevitable.

'The absolutely bewildering thing,' said one of the officers in his account, 'was the relative speed at which the ships passed each other in a vertical direction. The men waiting on the after promenade deck were forty feet above our fo'c'sle at one moment and at the next they were ten feet below it. They flashed past and had to jump as if they were jumping from an express lift.' The jumping had gone on for almost six hours. A few of the men had misjudged their leaps and had hurtled between the ships to be crushed and drowned. Many had broken arms and legs and others had been injured in falling across guard rails. Over one hundred and eighty men had been saved.

The story was an epic of effort and courage, impossible to comprehend. One read, tried to piece the true story together from experience and imagination. 'The seamanship of the destroyer Captain must have been of a masterly quality,' said Willoughby. 'Glad it wasn't *Tobias* that had to take the job on.'

These were but a few of the stories that were told. For each one that was printed, under explanatory official headings and captions, we knew that a hundred were lived and unrecorded: that for each tale of impossible endurance and resolution there were scores that could never be told. Through these pages we glimpsed briefly at the others in the unending Atlantic Battle and then turned to our own slight parts.

～❧

A voyage was almost ended. We came towards Skerryvore, that great rock set in the Western Approaches fifty miles from the Scottish mainland. Always the sight of the dim loom of its flashes gave a lilt to our hearts, and, I am sure, a keener light to our eyes. We were not yet home and many difficulties might still await us, but if we were torpedoed and escaped, we should not be in the great wastes of the ocean, but within *living* distance of our homeland, and with the thought the distant flashes became as homely and as comforting as a quilted tea cosy and I turned once more to time and count the nervous flickers at the world's edge, gaining a bearing, checking the ship's position on the chart, thanking once more that race of nineteenth-century engineers who had placed these mighty friendly lights about our coast. I recalled always, at the sight of the distant looming, an engraving in a Victorian book my Aunt Ruth had given me on my fourteenth birthday and which was amongst the few books that I kept on board. The engraving, 'to face page 28', sharp with Victorian detail and exactitude, showed comparisons of sections of Skerryvore and Bell Rock light towers. I can read again the pompous yet endearing description, for the book is in the shelf an arm's length from me. 'The tower on this rock,' says the author of *Our Seamarks*, 'was commenced by Mr Alan Stevenson in 1838 and completed in 1844. At an early stage in the operations Mr Stevenson erected a strong wooden barrack on the rock, but it was carried away in a storm. Another was built ...' and so on, a simple tale of great exertion, pompously told, and I told the tale to Willoughby to pass time on the bridge. As if to share my admiration for these Victorian supermen, Benson suddenly declaimed, 'The cubical measurement of the stone part of the tower is 58,580 feet, representing some 4,300 tons of masonry. The total cost of this great work amounted to no less than £90,268.'

We laughed. I remembered that he had borrowed the book from my shelf a few days before: it was typical of him that he should memorise the one paragraph which would earn him smiles upon the bridge. I taxed him with deliberate exhibitionism, but he chuckled in the darkness, saying, 'Not at all, Number One. Sheer mental exercise. Sort of personal Pelmanism.'

'You might apply some of it to your list of stores next time, Benson,' said the Captain. 'The personal touch was more evident than the Pelmanism in the last replacements list you put in at the base.'

'Aye, aye, sir,' said Alphabet. The Captain continued with the subject of lighthouses, contending that ninety thousand quid was a ridiculously low figure for a lighthouse, scarcely the price of a corvette.

'The Eddystone and Bell only cost sixty thousand apiece,' said Benson in his best guide-book manner, and then recited:

> A ruddy gleam of changeful light
> Bound on the dusky brow of night:
> The seaman bids my lustre hail,
> And scorns to strike his tim'rous sail.

'What drivel is that?' asked Willoughby.

'You do grave injustice to a great writer, sir,' said Alphabet. 'The lines were written by Sir Walter Scott in a visitors' book they used to keep in the Bell, but he was only a mister then.'

'Mister or title, he was a damn bad poet,' decided Willoughby. 'Did he really write ruddy?'

'So the book says.'

'I suppose if I didn't serve in a corvette I might say "ruddy" sometimes. Wonder how much Peter Scott paid for his lighthouse?'

'We might send a note as from *Tobias*,' I suggested. 'After all, he's in the RNVR.'

'He might think us inquisitive,' said the Captain, 'having missed the benefits of Benson's observations. Should we now direct our undivided attention to the convoy?' and we turned once more to consider the resolute silhouettes of tankers, merchantmen and a corvette moving serenely beneath the malignant moon. The seas moved crosswise to our course; my eyes could not leave the long tinselled path the thin moon made between our fleet; the wind moved keenly against my face, but we were nearly home and against that prospect the coldest wind would not prevail.

Willoughby, as if unable to escape from the subject of lighthouses, asked whether I knew what spells the keepers served. I conjectured one month, but ventured no knowledgeable estimate. The Captain was silent and then asked suddenly whether I had ever seen the play *Thunder Rock*. I had.

'I wonder whether many keepers are as queer as that chap in the play.'

'About the same percentage as queer sea captains,' I offered, and in the moonlight saw him turn slightly to discover personal reference in my guess, but I stared steadily ahead, waiting for his next remark.

'You're a reader, Number One. Why don't you read up the true histories of these lighthouse chaps. Must be a strange life. I quite see the escape idea of that playwright. I suppose we all get it sometime or another. Escaping to a lighthouse merely makes it more dramatic; I suppose that would be known as "good theatre". We tried to avoid "good theatre" in my documentary film outfit. I suppose we all want to escape. With most of us it's a vague idea that we'd like to go farming in Kenya or to the South Sea Islands in the Gauguin manner.'

He continued, musing aloud; seemingly obsessed with the idea of escape. I half-listened, but thought of the lives of the men securely set within the confines of their tower, wondering how war had impressed their lives. Perhaps very little: by day they would see great convoys moving towards or coming from the Western Ocean and often at night they would inevitably be aware that darkened convoys were moving beyond the looming of their lights. Their tasks were more important than ever before and it was certain that they continued in the great tradition, serving all mariners impartially, for U-boat commanders would know the Skerryvore signals as well as they knew the Flensburg lights. These thoughts wandered in my mind as I listened to Willoughby's surmises.

'This escape complex gets us all, sooner or later, Number One. It'll get you, too, one day. You may be very nicely placed as a typographer or whatever fancy name you give yourself, but one day you'll get the old urge and want to get away from it all ...', but I would not be drawn, saying only that the only escape which interested me was to escape from the Atlantic with all its dreary attendances.

'That's not escape, that's treason,' said the Captain. 'I daresay I could have you put in irons for that remark, Number One. Alphabet, what about some coffee?'

'Aye, aye, sir,' said Benson, and went. Within the bridge-house we were quiet, watching the Skerryvore light beyond the watchful convoy, the steady revolutions of our turbines the only noise in the great night.

❧

Yet I did escape from *Tobias* and from the Atlantic, for during our next run I caught a violent cold in Canada, allowed the cold to prosper into pneumonia during the return voyage, and in northern Ireland was taken ignominiously ashore on a stretcher, placed carefully within a naval ambulance and thence rushed to hospital.

There I remained for almost a month. At the end of that time a surgeon-commander, RN, deemed me unfit for sea service for six months, 'at least in those damn cockleshell corvettes', and bade me repair my strength somewhere in the English countryside at Their Lordships' expense.

I made one other visit to *Tobias*, tottering on board during my first days out of hospital, looking rather like a ghost from an Ulster cemetery. There was a great dinner in the old tradition. At the end of the meal I went to the Captain's cabin.

'You look tolerably green, Number One. What will you do?'

'I'm not to go near a corvette for six months,' I said.

'That's nothing but a prospect of pleasure.'

'It has its points, but now I feel mildly adrift.'

'D'you know what sort of job you want?'

'Not exactly.'

He wrote a name and department on a card. 'Drop a note to this chap. Tell him I suggested the idea. Mention your general background, omitting the more squalid sections. I understand he sometimes has quite good jobs in his gift.'

I read 'Lt-Commander H Stirling, RNVR, Naval Intelligence Division, Admiralty, SW1'.

We sat talking for two hours. I walked slowly back to the Grand Central and to my small room with Benson and Richmond. They argued about the merits of the new Number One. 'He's very efficient. I'll give you that,' said Benson, 'but so damned solemn. He says his father's a cleric. Can't believe that. My old man was a rector and I'm a typical son of a son of the manse.'

'He's solemn all right,' said Richmond. 'Wish he weren't so keen on the Left. I like being a minority of one. We don't have half so many wardroom arguments since you left, Number One, and yet you're not what I'd call the argumentative type.'

'Perhaps I merely stimulate arguments,' I suggested smugly, but they both guffawed.

A fortnight later, having received a reply from Stirling, I travelled to London and reported to the Admiralty. It would be difficult 'to snatch me from the clutches of the Director of Anti-Submarine Warfare,' he had written, but he outlined the nature of a job which would be available in a fortnight's time. The job sounded interesting, too interesting, in fact; there must be a catch somewhere, I thought as I waited to meet my prospective Chief and to hear of the job and the catch. The office in which I waited showed signs of the blitz; blackout fabric flapped within glassless window-frames; plaster was missing from the ceiling; the table and two chairs were bare, worn, strictly Civil Service in pattern. I felt no confidence in myself, hated my cell, and stood nervously to await my fate. Stirling came in with a Colonel of Royal Marines, in blue, red, gold. I was yet more deeply intimidated by the sudden entry of this pomp and splendour. Stirling made introductions and left.

The colonel was about fifty, of middle height, clean-shaven, shrewd-looking with wrinkled, humorous eyes. He stood as if on a quarterdeck, his back as straight as a pine tree. I could not take my eyes from his impeccable 'blues', and, although he was reassuringly informal, I was constrained and reticent, only too obviously bereft of any of those officer-like qualities which, if possessed, should be made immediately apparent, according to the best authorities. This is bad, I thought; I should have been gregarious in ports abroad, dined out more often in the wardrooms of battleships, met more marines (although the only battleship I had visited had not risen higher than a major amongst its 'jollies'), got around amongst the fleet. The colonel was, however, kind and mercifully straightforward.

'Stirling says he thinks you're the man for this job in my outfit,' said the colonel. 'He described the sort of thing, I suppose?'

I said yessir, dutifully, still rigid.

'I think you'll find it quite interesting. Of course, we're only in the early stages. Lot of trial and error stuff ahead, I should say. Anyway we all start from scratch. Good, we'll take it as settled. We work in Oxford, y'know. Report to me Monday morning. Get your warrants here. We'll fix you up for billets in one of the Colleges. Good. I think that's all.'

Thus briefly was my new career settled.

~❧

For a short time I resided in what were, I was quite certain, the coldest rooms in the University of Oxford, overlooking the quadrangle of a small fifteenth-century college. I was still regaining my strength, finding with the fury and fretfulness of the healthy how long it takes to recover from real sickness. I lived for a while an almost collegiate life. The college scout was as attentive and efficient as Jake Gibbs, although quieter, less likely to engage in a searching, highly articulate inquiry into the morals of his friends than that lively steward. The white, draughty college rooms, however, I reckoned poor exchange for the compact, utilitarian comfort of my cabin, and for a time I was given to self-pity and became morose in my fate, but there were beautiful buildings, bookshops and slowly growing friendships with a few university people; yet I had no great love for Oxford and I felt only relief when a few weeks later, I was deputed to go to London, there to continue my new tasks. The friends have remained and perhaps those friendships have developed in me a liking for Oxford, which I now visit with delight, no longer regarding the city as a synonym for ill-health and unhappiness.

The colonel's promise that my job would be interesting was an understatement. During the two succeeding years I was sent upon solitary missions to the United States, the Middle East and to the Far East. I was enabled to see much of the world at war and parts of the world on the touchlines of war. I saw many of the great, hustling cities of the New World, from Chicago to San Francisco, engaged upon their fantastic tasks of production by day, upon their fantastic pleasures by night;

I mixed with the immense armies of native and American workers in Pearl Harbor and lived with the navies and armies of the United States and Australia in the islands of the Pacific; I moved with a New Zealand division in the Western Desert and dined with wartime diplomats in Lisbon and Istanbul; I saw something of the resurgence of British power in India under Admiral Mountbatten's South-East Asia Command and more of the taut civil conflicts in Palestine and Syria. In writing these words I realise that I have probably seen and heard more than the war correspondents of great newspapers, yet, unlike those gentlemen, I have been permitted to keep my memories to myself, and in this exercise of comparative silence I count myself amongst the more fortunate of mortals.

I sometimes smiled to think that I had been put aside by the sea, but as if in some sardonic exchange I had been enabled to see more of this distracted globe than any amateur sailor. I had crossed the world's oceans and the great ports of the world had become familiar places to me but I had also moved beyond the seas and ports far inland, where no other sailors came: none of these things would now be amongst my memories had I remained in *Tobias*. I began to write this book two years ago in Alexandria, I remember, and I finish its slow course in a courtyard off Fleet Street. I have not known the sea in all that time, except as passenger. The war has ended, the battle of the Atlantic has ended, but it is well that we should never forget that battle. A month ago I saw in the great indestructible U-boat pens in Trondheim those craft which had been recently built to make that battle a more onerous and terrible experience for our seamen. Yet we are such a forgetful race. Sometimes, I think, there appears no hope that we shall ever learn from our lessons, however harsh those lessons are. Thirty thousand merchant seamen were killed in the war at sea, I read the other day, most of them in the Atlantic: and that total would be greatly swollen by Royal

Navy names. Let us not forget them: they lie in the narrow warm seas of the Caribbean, in the wide cold seas of the Arctic, off bare Nova Scotia and the wild Irish coast. It is not right or even well that we should forget again, for if we forget we do not deserve to live. We live by the sea, because of the sea and the sea must be always with us. 'A sermon by Number One, by God!' Willoughby would have said, yet it is scarcely that, but a simple truth of geography and history. Yet so many of our politicians seem ignorant of both those studies.

❧

My story is almost done, but the paragraphs which remain are difficult to write. During the months after I left *Tobias,* as I learned my new tasks and began to move about the world upon these tasks, I received long letters from Richmond and Benson, laconic postcards from Willoughby. His words were careless in calligraphy, brief in content. 'Dear ex,' he wrote. 'You seem to have found yourself a cushy numero. Don't work too hard and if you get to the Med, stay there. We are still on these ocean runs and still loathe them. If you dine at the Etoile let me know whether they still have smoked salmon's roe. Always a favourite of mine. Write often but at greater length than this. Richmond and Alphabet learn apace. I may leave soon. My name's down for a Hunt. The new Jimmy doesn't laugh as much as you did, but he's more efficient, needless to say. A mechanically-minded type. Dundass sends his love. Miles W.'

I was gladdened to hear that he might get his dream of a Hunt class destroyer. I had heard that a few RNVR officers were getting these commands: it would be fun to visit him on board, I thought, yet this was Willoughby's last note, for in the following month HMS *Tobias* was torpedoed and sunk in the North Atlantic. Willoughby, Benson, the Chief and more than half the crew were lost: Richmond and my successor as First Lieutenant were the only officers saved. I read the report, two months after the loss, whilst in the Middle East, in Beirut. I had been travelling and had not heard of her loss. In the naval mess in that pleasant port I picked up a tattered copy of *The Times* to read the month-old news, and turning the pages I noticed a naval Roll of Honour. Under the heading of HMS *Tobias*, 'the loss of which has previously been announced by the Admiralty', was a list of names, missing, believed killed. I read through the remembered names: Lt-Cmdr M R Willoughby, RNVR, Sub-Lieut K G W C Benson, RNVR, Warrant Officer H Dundass, RN, and then the others: Donovan, Gibbs, Hill, Jones, King, Mason, Mitchell, Myers, Osborne, and on and on through thirty-seven names. Only Richmond, from the wardroom group, it seemed, had been saved.

I sat in the wicker chair long after reading, numbed, saddened, lost in the impossibility of understanding that I should not meet my friends again. I knew that several corvettes had been sunk, but always one thinks one's own ship and shipmates will escape, in that same way, I suppose, that one always apportions immortality to oneself: only others die, are killed or missing. Now, too, I realised that in my mind, Willoughby had remained most clearly set aside as perhaps the only friend made in the war who had seemed destined to continue in friendship in the distant peace. Now I was slow in thought, unwishful to know that with the others he was gone, numbered with those many tombless dead the war had left within *the steep Atlantick stream*.

THE END

Alexandria 1943
London 1945